STONE WALL

Breaking Out in the Fight for Gay Rights

ANN BAUSUM

speak

SPEAK
An imprint of Penguin Random House LLC
375 Hudson Street
New York, New York 10014

First published in the United States of America by Viking,
an imprint of Penguin Young Readers Group, 2015
This edition published by Speak, an imprint of Penguin Random House LLC, 2016

THE LIBRARY OF CONGRESS HAS CATALOGED THE VIKING EDITION AS FOLLOWS:
Bausum, Ann.
Stonewall : breaking out in the fight for gay rights / Ann Bausum.
pages cm.
Summary: A dramatic retelling of the Stonewall riots of 1969, introducing teen readers
to the decades-long struggle for gay rights.
ISBN 978-0-670-01679-2 (hardcover)
[1. Stonewall Riots, New York, N.Y., 1969—Juvenile literature.
2. Gay liberation movement—United States—History—20th century—Juvenile literature.
3. Gay men—United States—History—20th century—Juvenile literature.
4. Lesbians—United States—History—20th century—Juvenile literature.]

Speak ISBN 978-0-14-751147-8

Printed in the United States of America

3 5 7 9 10 8 6 4 2

Cover: Marty Robinson (left) addresses a rally commemorating the Stonewall riots, July 27, 1969. "We've got to stand up," he urged. "This is our chance."

Dedicated to Mike Bess

Written in memory of
Tyler Clementi (1991–2010)
and
Michael Riesenberg (1958–1993)

∼ CONTENTS ∼

Members of the Gay Activists Alliance help form a human chain across the George Washington Bridge between New York and New Jersey to demonstrate their support for gay rights, May 6, 1973.

A PROLOGUE

Greenwich Village.

No, no, no. Not Green-witch. Drop the W. Drop an E.

Grenitch Village. Gren-itch. Got it?

Greenwich Village, 1969: Home to the homeless. Destination for drop-outs. Refuge for the kicked out.

Meet at The Corner. That's Greenwich Avenue and Sixth Avenue, opposite West Eighth Street. Everyone is there. To cruise. To chat. To find friends. Friends for life. Friends for a moment.

Walk up Sixth Avenue and you reach Fourteenth Street, the edge of the Village. Walk down Sixth, and you've left the Village when you cross Houston. (*No. Not Houston like "Houston, we have lift-off," not Houston like Houston, Texas. It's Houston as in How-ston. Got it?*) Cross Houston and you're in SoHo. Go back.

Go back toward The Corner, head east on Eighth Street, turn right at Fifth Avenue, and you'll find Washington Square Park. The heartbeat of the Village. Another hangout. There's the fountain and the namesake arch: "The event is in the hand of God." Open space. Green space. A space for hanging out.

Keep heading east and you stay in the Village. That's the East Village over there.

But back at The Corner, you're in the West Village. The place to be.

Don't miss Christopher Street. Born at The Corner. Headed toward the Hudson River, the western boundary of Manhattan. Walk to the water's edge and you've reached the trucks. More later about the trucks.

But first, retrace your steps. Follow the narrow street back to the breathing spot of Seventh Avenue South. Lots of streets meet here. Lots of open space celebrates the junctures. Even a park. Christopher Park. Easy to remember. Christopher Street. Christopher Park.

That door where people pause, then enter? Yes. That's important. Pay attention.

That's the Stonewall.

The Stonewall Inn.

Pay attention.

History walks through that door.

East Village rambler, New York City, November 12, 1967.

CHAPTER 1

FLASH POINT

> "The door of the Stonewall had wrought-iron bars across this little peephole, a little wooden thing that slid open. And the man inside would look at you and, if you looked like you belonged there, would let you in."
>
> —CHRIS BABICK,
> describing the entrance to the Stonewall Inn

FOR STARTERS, THERE WAS A FULL MOON. AND IT WAS beastly hot. Plus it was Friday night in New York City. A party night. A night to hit the bars, dance, and hang out with friends, even if the friends were gay. Especially if the friends were gay.

In the summer of 1969, the Stonewall Inn served as a space for gays to meet, dance together, and express their physical attractions. It provided a showplace for cross-dressers to camp it up in their finery. It was a spot to hang out with other people who understood what it felt like to be gay on the cutting edge of changing times.

On the street gays kept alert, wary of police officers in uniform and mindful that the next attractive stranger posing as a homosexual might in fact be an imposter packing a police badge. Every state

The façade of the Stonewall Inn (still marked by the graffiti of recent events), September 1969. Unrest three months earlier converted this spot in Greenwich Village into ground zero for gay rights history.

except Illinois carried sodomy laws that prohibited nonvaginal sexual intercourse, chiefly directed at gay men. People caught defying these laws—especially in public but even at home—could expect to land in jail and receive verbal abuse, or worse, on the way.

In the workplace gays lived on edge, too. With the exception of a few careers, such as theater work, most gays had to mask their sexual identities or risk being fired. It was perfectly legal to dismiss someone from a job because of perceived sexual deviance, and then homosexuality topped the list of so-called abnormal behavior. Federal employees, including armed service members, faced automatic discharge if they failed to conceal their sexual orientations. Prospects for employment elsewhere, and even for finding housing, became grim. "Why they don't just round us all up and kill us I don't know," lamented one discredited military veteran.

At home gays might not find much refuge, either. Most young gay men and lesbians felt compelled to live with the secret of being different. Perhaps they faced rejection, even being disowned, for admitting their attraction to same-sex partners. These youths often left home, either by choice or by order of disapproving parents, and they headed to urban centers in search of companionship and a hint of tolerance. Older gay men and lesbians might marry people of the opposite gender, either in an attempt to combat their same-sex urges or because they sought the legitimizing shelter of marriage, but peace of mind could rarely be found in such relationships.

Whether on the street, at work, or at home, gays confronted the reality that acting on their sexual orientations constituted illegal behavior. Any portrayal of homosexuality in the media tended to reinforce these negative stereotypes. After all, such actions ran counter to the teachings of organized religion. A homosexual life was a sinful life, many clergy members preached. Anyone living openly as a homosexual could expect eternal damnation in the afterlife and was unlikely to be welcomed to worship.

Meanwhile, the medical community condemned homosexuals

as mentally ill. To overcome thoughts and behaviors judged to be deviant, doctors advised intensive talk therapy, even electroshock treatment. Some gay men were castrated against their will, a procedure that removed their testicles and deadened the sex drive. Others were lobotomized, a medical practice that destroyed the connections between the frontal lobes and the thalamus of the brain, deadening just about all aspects of behavior.

Gays who settled in such urban centers as New York City and San Francisco knew that the best place to find understanding and camaraderie was with other gays. In New York City, the southwestern neighborhood of Manhattan known as Greenwich Village served as a magnet for many gay men and lesbians. Its reputation pulled gay runaways and adults alike to a city where many found the closest thing that could pass for a safe community.

Gay bars served as natural places to meet in such neighborhoods, and, as hangouts went, these establishments felt relatively safe. No one performed lobotomies there, and no one condemned the patrons as sinners. If gays were lucky, no one arrested them either. For all the plusses, during the 1960s gay bars in New York City came with plenty of negatives. Many were run by the organized crime syndicate of the Mafia. Bouncers might refuse to let patrons enter. Overpriced drinks featured watered-down alcohol to boost profits. Sanitary practices might be nonexistent, from the bar counters to the bathrooms. Police routinely raided the bars, both to enforce laws that prohibited various aspects of homosexual behavior and to reinforce a system of payoffs by Mafia owners to corrupt police officers. But something was better than nothing, so gays who wanted to socialize flocked to the bars that sheltered them from public scrutiny and offered them the comfort of camaraderie.

The Stonewall Inn (which was a bar only, not a hotel, despite its name) had a rough-and-tumble character from the time it opened in 1967. It stood on Christopher Street, a vibrant east-west corridor that cut through the heart of the West Village. Its building had housed everything from a stable to a French bakery to a tearoom to a burned-out restaurant before it debuted as a gay bar.

Bouncers at the Stonewall literally screened patrons by peering through a vertical slit in the door. The three-dollar price of weekend admission included two free drinks, albeit ones of suspect cleanliness and integrity. (Weekday admission cost one dollar.) The grungy bathrooms drew use only from patrons in desperate need of a toilet. Its bars didn't even have sinks to wash dirty glasses. The whole place had a subterranean, primitive feel. Barricaded windows. Black walls. Minimal furnishing. Dark. Smelly, with whiffs of cologne and perfume and body odor wafting off of patrons. And, like all bars then, a film of cigarette smoke clouding the air.

None of that mattered, though, because the Stonewall Inn had something not always found at gay bars: music. Plenty of music, and twin dance floors. Few bars in New York, even gay bars, permitted same-sex dancing, but the Stonewall's dance floors were open to all. Patrons dropped coins into the jukeboxes and lost themselves in the beat of a popular song, the crush of bodies on the dance floor, and the freedom of physical interaction between same-sex couples. For many of the patrons, the Stonewall offered one of those rare places where they felt like they belonged.

The late 1960s pushed all sorts of social boundaries in the United States, especially for young people. A vibrant youth subculture arose, and its followers experimented with illegal drugs, fed the development of popular music, protested an unpopular war in Vietnam, and embraced, literally, the sexual freedoms fueled by the whole scene. Thousands of young people had frolicked in San Francisco during 1967 in what was dubbed the Summer of Love. Gays were as interested in the grand experiment as straight people, and the Stonewall Inn offered the homosexual equivalent to many heterosexual hangouts. Rich with grunge. Loose in spirit. Full of bodies, a relentless drumbeat, and abundant alcohol.

Who went to the Stonewall? Representatives of the full

A participant in the Summer of Love in San Francisco, June 21, 1967. The Stonewall Inn had opened as a gay bar just months earlier. Two years later, thanks in part to the countercultural influence of events such as the Summer of Love, the Stonewall would explode with activism.

spectrum of gay expression. Closeted males with respectable jobs and reputations seeking a discreet way to express their same-sex preferences. Married men acting on their desires to be physically involved with other men. Runaway youths, drawn by New York's gay scene, who hung together on the streets of Manhattan and partied together at the Stonewall. Artists, performers, and intellectuals who lived openly as gays. A few straight friends of gays.

In 1969 the legal drinking age in New York was eighteen, so plenty of the young people who frequented the Stonewall either were legal or could pass for it. Most Stonewall patrons were in their teens and twenties. Few were over forty. Men constituted the vast majority of patrons at the Stonewall, but lesbians visited it sometimes, too. So did men who proudly called themselves queens, adopting feminine mannerisms and, on occasion, wearing women's clothing. Such individuals were labeled transvestites, drag queens, and cross-dressers during an era before the existence of the broader term *transgender*. Many toggled between genders, wearing men's clothing sometimes and taking on female personas and appearance at others.

"It was the best place we ever had."

—DICK KANON, describing the Stonewall Inn in 1969

Time passed in three-minute intervals at the Stonewall, give or take a few seconds. Cue "Satisfaction" by the Rolling Stones (3 minutes, 44 seconds). Maybe Diana Ross and the Supremes sang "Stop! In the Name of Love" (2 minutes, 52 seconds). Or the Beach Boys harmonized on "I Get Around" (2 minutes, 12 seconds). Song by song, dance by dance, the evening spun away.

Visitors split their time between the bar's two main rooms. The front room, adjacent to Christopher Street, drew the older and more conventional customers. This space housed the main bar plus side tables. A dance floor dominated the room, driven by a jukebox stocked with pop tunes. Ten cents bought one song; a quarter paid for three. Dancers weaved in and out of spotlight beams, performing for the crowd. Men danced with men, often for the first time in their lives. By 1969, a pair of scantily clad go-go boys had added their professional moves to the dance beat from within the set of matching cages that bookended the bar.

The Stonewall's back room held a dance floor, too. In fact, the dance floor served as the main feature of the back room, although the space did have its own small bar and limited perimeter seating. This room drew the younger patrons, perhaps in part because the back room's jukebox offered a playlist of raw blues, Motown hits, and gutsy soul music that addressed conflicts relevant to their youthful lives. The greatest ethnic and visual diversity appeared in the back room, too, with African Americans, Puerto Ricans, and whites, some in drag, mixing into an exotic canopy of free expression.

On June 27, 1969, the Stonewall Inn pulsed to the beat of the music, pulsed to the beat of hundreds of hearts, pulsed to the beat of the final year in a tumultuous decade. "There was a generally up mood in the place," one chronicler later recalled. An up mood "as friends who hadn't seen one another for at least twenty-four hours were reunited in deeply felt embrace, as newfound lovers exchanged meaningful kisses on the dance floor or across a table, while others sipped their drinks waiting for Prince Valiant to come."

Waiting and dancing. Waiting and dreaming. Waiting.

An up mood. A hot night. A full moon hanging outside. The pulse of changing times. Times when anything could happen. Midnight. Twelve thirty. One twenty a.m.

And then the overhead lights came alive. Dancers froze in the brightness as the jukeboxes ceased to blast the night's beat. Person by person, awareness dawned through the fog of smoke and sweat and booze.

R-a-i-d.

RAID.

CHAPTER 2

THE CLOSET

"When you left bars you always had to stiffen up and look straighter and try to be always on your guard. Just walking with my friends down the street from one bar to another was a heavy thing." —PERRY BRASS,

recollecting the gay bar scene
in New York City during the 1960s

CRAIG RODWELL WASN'T AT THE STONEWALL INN DURING the raid on that hot night in June 1969, but he could have been. Rodwell had arrived in New York City a decade earlier, one of countless displaced young men drawn to Greenwich Village. Initially he had visited the clubs and hangouts popular with the city's gay community. By 1969, though, at age twenty-eight, he had become an outspoken critic of the gay bars in Greenwich Village— or at least the Mafia-run gay bars, which pretty much meant all the gay bars in the area.

Being outspoken had become one of Rodwell's trademarks. His outspokenness had gotten him arrested and jailed in 1962 after he objected to police harassment over his wearing a skimpy swimsuit

Early gay rights activists Randy Wicker and Barbara Gittings participate in an Independence Day protest for gay rights in Philadelphia, 1966.

popular with gays. His outspokenness had put him on protest lines since 1965 in support of fair treatment for homosexuals. And his outspokenness had led him in 1967 to found the Oscar Wilde Memorial Bookshop, the nation's first bookstore devoted to gay literature.

Rodwell had arrived in New York to become a ballet dancer.

Craig Rodwell at Riis Park beach in New York City, circa 1961.

Instead he'd become a radical. In between he'd tried to find his fit in the world as a gay man. Many of his early experiences took him out on the streets of New York City. In the late 1950s and early 1960s he'd run with a crowd of other gay teens. He and his friends wore the era's signature fashion for rebellious youths: blue jeans. For Rodwell's crowd, the tighter the jeans the better. "We couldn't have them tight enough. Literally. We used to wash our jeans," he explained, "soak them in hot water," to shrink them down for a snugger fit.

Often when they went out on the town, Rodwell and his friends added eyeliner and mascara to their eyes, deliberately marking themselves as gay. It was a gesture of defiance. "Going wrecking," they called it. Rodwell and company enjoyed the shock value their behavior had on the groups of straight teens who likewise toured the streets of the city. "Just holding hands in front of them, swishing by them, and being outrageous, upsetting them," explained Rodwell. Such daring behavior could have provoked attacks or arrests, but the reward of startled reactions among straight bystanders made up for the risks. Acting out also probably helped to release some of the anger and frustration that built from being treated as outsiders.

On some occasions the teens added music to their performance art. Standing shoulder to shoulder, they borrowed the tune from the opening theme song of a popular children's television program, *Howdy Doody*. Discarding the show's official lyrics, the youths converted its "Ta-ra-ra boom-de-ay" melody into their own unofficial anthem. Locked arm in arm, their voices aligned, the youths high-kicked to the beat and sang:

> *We are the Village queens.*
> *We always wear blue jeans.*
> *We wear our hair in curls,*
> *Because we think we're girls.*

Such antics and companionship helped balance the challenges of living openly as a gay person during an era when few people did. Years later, Rodwell's contemporary Jerry Hoose recollected his own introduction to life in the West Village. He reached what locals called "The Corner," at Sixth Avenue and Eighth Street, and "found Nirvana. There were all these drag queens and these crazy people and everybody was carrying on. I made friends that first day." Hoose characterized those gays who, like himself, refused to hide their same-sex preferences as the "have-nothing-to-lose types."

Many of them were homeless. Plenty were scarred by discrimination. Some bore literal scars. Blister-scarred faces. Branded buttocks. Burn-marked forearms. These marks told the stories of parents so horrified to learn that their sons loved men that they had resorted to extreme measures. Better to be seared by a hot iron. Better to be scalded and scarred by boiling water. It was far better, thought these most judgmental of parents, to be branded in this lifetime than to burn in hell for all eternity.

The youthful outcasts lived a hardscrabble life, stealing, turning tricks as hustlers, turning on one another out of frustration, turning for relief to drugs, turning up dead. The most visible and marginalized homosexuals adopted street names and spoke using an insider's code about people called Miss Thing and Opera Jean, or Congo Woman, Mary Queen of Scotch, and Captain Faggot. These individuals, though male, might be addressed as "she" and be described as "nelly."

Street-savvy gays devised code words for their number one enemy, too. "Here comes Lillian," they'd warn, when a police officer came into view. Lillian, as in Lilly Law. Otherwise known as Betty Badge. Or Patty Pig. (It was, after all, an era when just about every counterculture person around—straight or gay—derisively referred to police officers as pigs.)

Lillian came around a lot in New York City during the 1960s because society and prejudice gave police officers many excuses to persecute homosexuals. For starters, masquerading in the attire of the opposite sex was a criminal offense, except on Halloween. Local law required individuals to wear at least three gender-appropriate articles of inner and outer clothing at all times, a policy that confounded the wardrobe planning of cross-dressers. As Martin Boyce later joked about the requirements for men: "Mind you socks didn't count, so it was underwear, and undershirt—now the next thing was going to ruin the outfit."

Most gay men did dress in male attire, but that didn't protect them while they were engaged in another practice that attracted a lot of police attention: cruising. Gay men cruised particular sections of the city in search of everything from instant sexual partners to long-term lovers. Police officers regularly cruised alongside them. Crowds of gay men would walk past one another at The Corner, or by a stretch of benches along Central Park West. Billy-club-wielding patrols shadowed their steps. "Keep moving, faggot, keep moving," the police might chide, sometimes literally poking the pedestrians in the ribs with their wooden weapons.

An alternative to street cruising was the truck scene along the western edge of lower Manhattan. Pushed out of the parks, flushed from the city's streets, gays found refuge in the unlocked trailers of semi trucks parked by the banks of the Hudson River. By day the trucks harbored animal carcasses en route from slaughterhouses to meat markets. By night the trucks sat emptied of everything but the stench of dead flesh, creating a noxious but sheltered space for sexual encounters. Visitors might find hundreds of men packed into one trailer, with hundreds more in adjacent units. But Lilly Law and Patty Pig patrolled this part of town, too, stripping even this haunt of real security.

Bars and other establishments that catered to members of the gay community offered no guarantee of sanctuary at the beginning of the 1960s, either. Local authorities interpreted state laws to mean that homosexuals were inevitably disorderly and thus could not legally be served alcohol. Some bars literally posted signs that read, "If You're Gay, Go Away." Identifying the homosexuals in a crowd could be challenging, however. Flamboyant cross-dressers were easy to spot, but they were an exception within the gay community. Plenty of people might live as gay men and lesbians but look like heterosexuals.

Police officers practiced the art of entrapment to tease the offending gays out of the crowd. These officers left their Lilly Law attire behind and dressed as civilians. Then they stepped into gay bars and tried to trick someone of the same gender into expressing an interest in having sex. The New York City police force pursued this practice with enthusiasm, both inside bars and at cruising spots. By the 1960s their pursuit was so systematic that they would sometimes convert a convenient hotel room into a guarded makeshift holding pen, allowing the undercover officers to return swiftly to the streets and bars in search of more catches. When the hotel room was full, officers called it a night and transferred their haul to their precinct headquarters for official processing.

The ongoing repression of the gay community created opportunities for corruption during a time when organized crime, spearheaded by the Mafia from its bases in Italy and New York City, intersected with many segments of commerce. New York's Mafia operatives realized that the city's homosexual community represented an untapped commercial market. Thus the Mafia began to open gay bars using a wink-and-nod system with corruptible members of the city's police force. Police officers ignored the illegal clubs as long as Mafia managers diverted a share of the proceeds to members of the force.

Periodic police raids of Mafia-run gay bars usually indicated that someone hadn't been making payments as promised. Sometimes raids were conducted to keep up an appearance of the rule of law and order, but bar owners were often tipped off in advance, thus limiting the raids' impact. Gay patrons became so familiar with the patterns that they knew to expect more raids during an election season (when crime crackdowns earned voter support), and they came to recognize the cozy relationships observed between bar managers and local police officers as the tip of an iceberg of corruption.

Rejected as social outcasts. Harassed by the authorities. Forced to hide their feelings. Such realities created a dilemma. Individuals could be true to themselves and be revealed as gay, or they could conceal their true identities and preserve access to the lifestyle of the straight world. Neither option was ideal. Most gays found it safest to keep their sexual orientations private, with the possible exception of discreet sharing among like-minded comrades. Living in the closet, it came to be called. Living in the closet.

The prospect of a tortured future could feel like a death sentence, and suicide rates ran higher among the gay population then, as now. Even Craig Rodwell reached a tipping point where the burden of living as a gay man seemed unbearable. His lover, a successful businessman named Harvey Milk, disapproved of

Rodwell's activism because it conflicted with Milk's need to keep his sexuality a secret so that he wouldn't lose his job. A decade later, Milk would move to San Francisco and transform himself into one of the most noted gay political leaders of all time, but in 1962 Rodwell's defiance was out of sync with his partner's need for privacy. Milk stepped back from their relationship, and Rodwell decided to end his life with a drug overdose. Only the unexpected return of a roommate kept his plan from succeeding.

"The closet door was so tight back then."

—DANNY GARVIN, recollecting the era of the 1960s and before

Those who resisted the path of suicide—or tried it and survived—did their best to bear the weight of oppression and the self-imposed silence that often accompanied same-sex preferences. This very anonymity made it that much harder to fight back against injustices. If you remained silent and anonymous, how could you fight your oppression? If you remained silent and anonymous, how could you ever overcome the weight that came with that most private of choices: whom to love?

After surviving his suicide attempt, Rodwell doubled down on activism. He expanded his participation in a small but vibrant movement for gay rights that had started on the West Coast and spread to other parts of the country. Members of such early organizations as the Mattachine Society (founded by gay men) and the Daughters of Bilitis (organized by lesbians) introduced the term *homophile* to describe themselves, preferring it over *homosexual*, a word that carried a heavy dose of judgment. The groups created publications to raise awareness within the gay community, and representatives began to advocate for their rights, sometimes collaborating across gender lines.

Although lesbians shared many of the same concerns as gay men—from police crackdowns to mental illness labels to condemnation as sinners—they faced additional barriers due to enduring patterns of discrimination against women. This reality forced lesbians to fight battles on two fronts, first as women weary of oppression and reduced opportunity, and second as outsiders from the accepted norm of heterosexuality. Those who were women of color faced even more discrimination and challenge.

Gay men didn't automatically possess sympathy for the lesbian point of view, because being gay didn't necessarily make a man more sensitive to the challenges lesbians faced in the world. Gay men could be just as chauvinistic, just as blind to the confining stereotypes of the era as their heterosexual contemporaries. They might assume, just as straight men typically did, that women were the designated coffee makers at meetings, that women were best left to doing clerical work, that women were meant to be followers, not leaders. Thus gay men and lesbians walked a fine line during their early quests for equality, sometimes collaborating as allies and sometimes at odds as adversaries.

The initial activism of these advocates for gay rights was heavily influenced by the nonviolent foundation of the ongoing African-American civil rights movement. Homophiles began staging similarly styled protests, starting with a cluster of picket marches at key landmarks in Washington, D.C., during the spring of 1965. Craig Rodwell was among the New Yorkers who traveled to participate in protests that an activist named Frank Kameny had helped to organize. "I was just so excited," Rodwell later recalled. "It was the most wonderful day in my life, marching in front of the White House in the open." But Rodwell became despondent when the series of spring picket marches ended. "This was the last one—there were no plans for anything else—I just couldn't bear that." On the spot he imagined a way to continue the protests on an annual basis. "Let's do it on July 4th at Independence Hall [in Philadelphia]. We'll do it every year," Rodwell proposed to the other activists. "I'm going to create a gay holiday," he thought.

On July 4, 1965, Rodwell's dream began to take form. Representatives of the various East Coast homophile organizations gathered in Philadelphia for what became known as the Annual Reminder protest. The event featured some fifty men and women who walked in a circle in front of Independence Hall carrying signs promoting the cause of homosexual equality. Borrowing an early tactic of the African-American civil rights movement, the marchers complied with a dress code of impeccable neatness and propriety. Men wore suits and ties. Women wore dresses or skirts, not pants. The idea was to make homosexuals look no different from heterosexuals, reinforcing the idea that they deserved to be treated equally.

As planned, the picketers returned in 1966 and subsequent years. Debates arose over the dress code, but coordinator Kameny insisted on absolute order. March in single file. No public displays of affection. No talking. Stay in line so that signs appear in

Gay activist Frank Kameny (right) fields questions from news reporters and onlookers during the Annual Reminder protest in Philadelphia, circa 1966.

the designated sequence. "Homosexuals Are American Citizens Also," proclaimed one marcher's sign in 1966. "Homosexuals Ask for Equality, Opportunity, Dignity," read another. "Stop Cruel and Unusual Punishment for Homosexuals," added a third mute participant while following the circular path of silent protest.

In the spring of 1966, Rodwell was among the members of the Mattachine Society of New York who borrowed another play from the African-American civil rights manual when they staged what the media dubbed a "Sip-In." Their action mirrored the sit-in protests that had begun in the American South in 1960. In this case four gay men elected to visit a series of New York bars and restaurants, testing their willingness to serve the men regardless of their sexual orientation. Declaring themselves to be orderly homosexuals, the men sat down and asked for drinks. The publicity and scrutiny that followed their effort forced the state of New York to declare that homosexuals could not be refused service of alcohol. Further challenges led to the assertion that gays could even dance together in public establishments.

The progress of gay rights, as with other social justice movements, was not linear. One set of gains could easily trigger pushback from opponents that led to losses, or further fighting, or burnout. But battles and gains also inspired further activism. "Gay Is Good" became the activists' motto. In 1967, Rodwell expressed his enthusiasm for the homophile movement by opening his bookstore in tribute to the nineteenth-century Irish author who had been jailed for being a homosexual. No one had ever seen a store like it before. This Greenwich Village hangout offered literature by and about homosexuals and established an atmosphere of openness and tolerance for the gay community.

Dissatisfied with the intermittent activism of Mattachine, Rodwell established an alternative organization, too. He called his group HYMN, short for Homophile Youth Movement in Neighborhoods, and began publishing a newsletter that he called the *Hymnal.* Rodwell didn't measure his success by membership; he measured it by impact. Soon young people were writing to him for advice, for counsel, for information, for inspiration. He nurtured them and encouraged them all to advocate, as he did, that Gay Is Good.

Such thinking proved challenging for older generations of homosexuals who had struggled for decades under the judgment of mental illness. The idea that they could be both gay and good "created quite a stir," recalled Rodwell during the filming of the 1984 documentary *Before Stonewall.* "It's hard for young people today [that is, in 1984] to imagine as little as twenty years ago a hundred gay people sitting around arguing over whether or not they should say that they weren't mentally ill."

Rodwell kept waiting for a spark to catch hold, for something to trigger a mass movement of advocacy for gay rights. He could sense that momentum was building for some sort of action. But old patterns die hard. In the late 1960s, straight citizens who bothered to think about homosexuals at all generally disapproved of them. The media mostly ignored both them and their efforts to gain greater respect. Police officers continued to taunt and harass them even after prohibitions were lifted against drinking and dancing in public places.

It was an era of riots and demonstrations, an era of clashes with the police. Clashes over the Vietnam War, over racial oppression, and even, on the West Coast, over police harassment of homosexuals. As the decade progressed toward its finale, the growing sentiment seemed to be, when faced with oppression, don't put up with it anymore.

Take the fight to the streets.

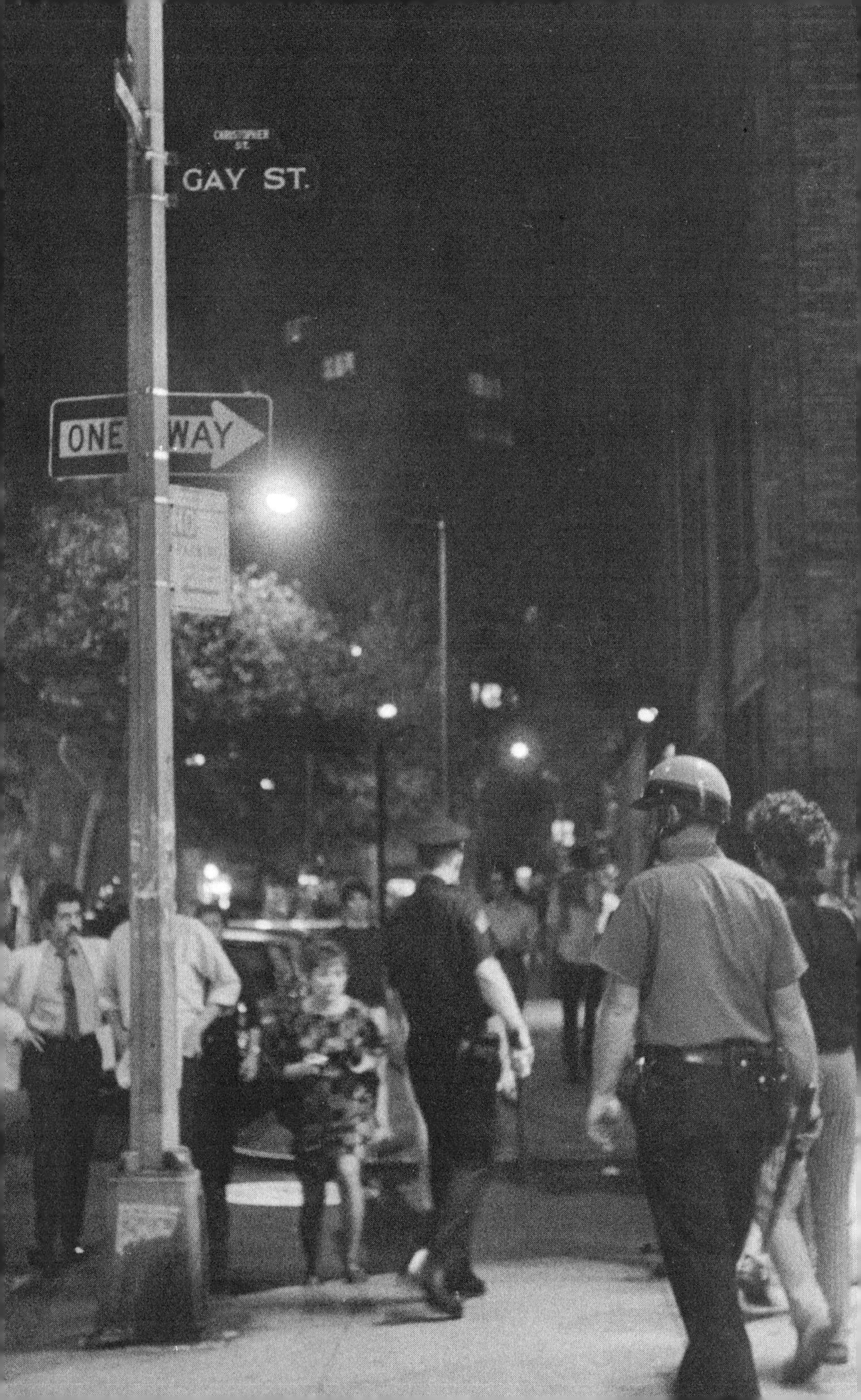
CHRISTOPHER ST.
GAY ST.
ONE WAY

CHAPTER 3

SHUT IT DOWN

> *"For me, there was no bar like the Stonewall, because the Stonewall was like the watering hole on the savannah. You know, it's just, everybody was there. We were all there."*
> —MARTIN BOYCE,
> recollecting the social scene at the Stonewall Inn

THE STONEWALL INN HAD BEEN IN BUSINESS FOR JUST OVER two years when Inspector Seymour Pine received his orders to close it down. This time the reason wasn't the old logic of it being criminal to serve alcohol to homosexuals. Nor was it the fact that homosexuals congregated there and danced together. New York's courts had ruled that neither of those behaviors broke any state laws. This time the reason came down to one word: blackmail.

International authorities had alerted New York's police department about suspicious sales in Europe of negotiable bonds that could be traced back to the United States. Could city authorities investigate the matter? Pine served as a deputy inspector for the New York Police Department in its public morals section, the sector responsible for enforcing state and local statutes dealing

Police officers patrol the Stonewall neighborhood, July 2, 1969.

Police officers patrol MacDougal Street in the West Village, March 19, 1966. They periodically tried to rid the streets of people who were considered undesirable, such as the homeless, prostitutes, and homosexuals.

with behavior. He and a police detective named Charles Smythe collaborated on cases that occurred in lower Manhattan, home to Greenwich Village.

In the spring of 1969 this pair learned that many of the American bonds could be traced to closeted homosexuals who worked in New York City's financial district. Organized crime operatives from the Mafia had apparently learned of the men's sexual orientation and, knowing that the revelation of this secret would result in job dismissals, had begun blackmailing them. The victims of this extortion began stealing bonds to pay the required hush money. Where had these men been marked? All signs pointed to the gay bars in Greenwich Village. The Stonewall Inn, one of the largest and most enduring, looked like the center of the web of corruption. Shut it down, Pine and Smythe were told. Eliminate this opportunity for blackmailing.

Tony Lauria, otherwise known as Fat Tony, had opened the

Stonewall Inn as a gay bar on March 18, 1967. Three childhood friends—characters nicknamed Zookie, Tony the Sniff, and Joey—had joined him as partners, along with a neighborhood Mafia boss known as Matty the Horse. That winter, as workers began covering the fire-scarred interior of the former Stonewall Inn Restaurant with black paint, the legality of welcoming homosexuals to a bar remained in question. Days before the Stonewall Inn opened for business, the chairman of the New York State Liquor Authority had admitted that no laws on the books explicitly prohibited homosexuals from being served alcohol in public establishments. Public dancing by homosexuals remained a question of debate until a judge's ruling in January of 1968 declared that, as Craig Rodwell later put it, there was "nothing illegal, per se, about a gay bar."

Even though the Stonewall Inn broke no laws in 1969, the bar had legal vulnerabilities. Proving that the place was the center of a blackmailing scheme might be hard to do. Proving that it didn't have a proper liquor license? That was easy. Because the Stonewall Inn had opened during a period of legal transition, Lauria had used a technical loophole to assure he could not be closed for serving homosexuals. Instead of opening a traditional bar, he had opened a bottle club. Unlike a public bar—technically open to anyone of age who fit the definition of orderly—a bottle club was considered to be a private, members-only establishment. As such, the Stonewall was subject to a different, less invasive set of regulations, ones that permitted the creation of a place that would attract homosexuals.

The Stonewall Inn maintained the façade of a bottle club by restricting entrance only to those individuals who made it past the club's bouncer. Furthermore, management charged a flat fee to those admitted and required them to sign a sort of registration book before proceeding to the bar. Bottles of liquor bore random "customer" names to make them look as if they were reserved for specific individuals. For added protection of this business model, the Stonewall management established the usual Mafia payoff system with corrupt local police officers. In exchange for weekly payments of cash, Lilly Law agreed to leave the Stonewall Inn alone.

During the late 1960s, the Mafia dominated New York's gay bar (and bottle club) business while city and state authorities tried to sort out what was legal and what was not. Profits were tremendous: the Stonewall Inn reportedly grossed five or six thousand dollars each Friday and Saturday night, the equivalent of about $35,000 per weekend night today. The math couldn't have been better; these establishments had limited expenses thanks to ready access to stolen goods—from cigarettes to alcohol—which could instantly be converted into merchandise.

Arguably the club's largest single expense was the money it paid police officers in exchange for protection from the crackdowns that continued while gay bars transitioned toward legality. Stonewall historian David Carter speculates that the bar's managers designated $1,200 a month for such payments, an amount equal in buying power to almost $8,000 today. The bar's profits made such a sum easy to afford.

By 1969, the two-year-old Stonewall Inn had evolved to keep up with the times. Enhanced lighting and the introduction of caged male go-go dancers added elements of hip culture to the already popular music and dancing. An illegal drug culture was on the rise nationally, and Mafia-run establishments offered easy access to the latest in-demand pills and substances. The establishment remained grungy, dark, and smoky, but it continued to serve as a magnet in the gay community, particularly for young males, including marginalized populations of street youths, effeminate men, and cross-dressing males. Patrons danced in packed proximity on the weekends. Some visitors noted that the bar's one-entrance layout made it a catastrophic fire trap in case of an emergency, but the chance to boogie to the tunes of Stevie Wonder, the Shangri-Las, Otis Redding, and other popular recording artists trumped concerns over safety.

"There's a certain hastiness about the look of the place. It seems to have only recently been converted from a garage into a cabaret; in about eight hours and at a cost of under fifty dollars."

—*THE HOMOSEXUAL HANDBOOK*, describing the Stonewall Inn, 1969

On Tuesday, June 24, 1969, Inspector Pine and Detective Smythe began collecting evidence against the Stonewall in an evening raid. By this point the pair had already succeeded at raiding and closing several other gay bars in Greenwich Village, and their visit to the Stonewall, albeit unwelcomed, had gone smoothly. Their haul from the night's visit included a number of employees and the establishment's stash of liquor. This evidence would help build the case that the Stonewall Inn wasn't really a bottle club and was operating without a proper license. If they could close the establishment on those grounds, they'd have shut down another avenue for Mafia blackmailing.

Pine knew it would take more than one visit to put the Stonewall out of business, and he began planning his next raid. However, his raid-'em-till-they-close strategy failed to anticipate other factors that threatened his plans. For starters, there was the bar's popularity. Even the Tuesday-night raid had been disruptive to Stonewall regulars. Gay bar patrons had thought the era of raids was fading. After all, drinking and dancing were now legal for New York's gays. Yet here they were, caught in a seeming time warp while other oppressed groups, such as women and African Americans, seemed to be gaining greater access to equality. In contrast, homosexual acts remained illegal in all but one state in the country. The younger and more marginalized patrons at the Stonewall felt such unfairness keenly, and these living-on-the-edge/nothing-to-lose people were plentiful, plenty mad, and street savvy.

No one had to look very far to find a target for this anger: The cops. Lilly Law. Betty Badge. Anger at the police had reached epidemic levels by the late 1960s within that generation of activists and radicals who protested everything from discrimination to racial oppression to political corruption and the Vietnam War. Who was it that inevitably stepped in to stop the protesters and enforce the status quo? The police. To push back against the calls for change? The police. To shut down even peaceful protests? The police. Fire hoses in Birmingham during the children's marches of 1963, battles in ghettos during race riots in cities across the country, the clubbing of protesters outside the 1968 Democratic National Convention in Chicago—during an era when law enforcement included a generous dose of tear gas, brutality, and bloodshed, it became easy to view the police as an enemy.

Inspector Pine's plan to return to the Stonewall meant he would be reentering this favored haunt at a time of increasing tension and resentment. His plan to return that Friday night meant the place would be busier than it had been on Tuesday. His plan to arrive after midnight meant the club would be packed, and, by that time of night, the club's patrons would have had plenty of time to pick their party poison, be it alcohol, pills, or marijuana. Although the night's full moon may merely have been a coincidental circumstance, the unseasonably hot weather on June 27, 1969, added one more reason for irritability among revelers and police alike.

Stonewall historian David Carter emphasizes how the bar's location and surrounding geography made it uniquely qualified to become a tinderbox for gay rights. The bar lay nestled in the heart of the West Village. Although Christopher Street and most neighboring streets were narrow, one-way roads that predated automobile traffic by centuries, the bar was within sight of Seventh Avenue South and a brief walk from Sixth Avenue, two

Police confront anti-war protesters with force in Chicago, August 26, 1968. Demonstrations against the Vietnam War resulted in street violence during that year's Democratic National Convention.

of Manhattan's major north-south thoroughfares. Furthermore, the West Village neighborhood sat above a teeming tangle of subway tracks that connected its residents to eight separate subway lines at two nearby stations, each of which had multiple entrances and offered ready access to and from other parts of the city. All this transportation made for a lot of foot traffic, and a lot of these pedestrians were gay.

In 1969, pay phones—coin-operated public telephones—were an essential form of communication. Drop in a dime, dial seven numbers, and hope that someone answered. Mobile phones, of course, were barely imaginable beyond the world of James Bond. Mechanical voice-mail answering machines wouldn't appear on the scene until the 1980s. Friends relied on planning, chance, and pay phones to stay connected. Anyone near the Stonewall had plenty of access to pay phones: as a pedestrian and transportation hub, it merited a corresponding network of communication lines.

In terms of geography, the Stonewall rested amidst a maze of streets that only a resident could love, or at least that only a resident could negotiate with confidence. Streets ran at angles. Streets ran one way. Streets ran the other way. Streets named West Fourth intersected with streets named West Tenth and West Thirteenth, a cartographic impossibility on any traditional grid of city blocks. Streets near the Stonewall could be one block long. Streets might even be one block long but bend midway at an odd angle, as did Gay Street, a narrow road intersecting with Christopher Street that had been named not for homosexuals but for a man who had led an anti-slavery riot in 1834.

Two small parks punctuated this confusing web of pavement. One lay across the street from the Stonewall Inn. This triangle of space marked the spot of a deadly tenement fire and bore the name Christopher Park. For reasons long since lost to the general public, the neighboring Sheridan Park, also triangular in shape, was not the home of the neighborhood's statue of Union Civil War hero General Philip Sheridan. Instead Sheridan commanded the terrain of Christopher Park, turf that served in the late 1960s as a popular hangout for gay street youth.

It probably wasn't on Inspector Pine's mind as he prepared to return to the Stonewall, but plenty of gays were attuned to the news of the city's latest homophobic incident at another park in New York City. The week before Pine's initial Stonewall raid, a group of citizens in the neighboring borough of Queens had become frustrated with the use of their local park as a spot for homosexual cruising and intercourse. After the band of vigilantes failed in their efforts to personally evict the men from the wooded site, they returned and cut down the trees and undergrowth that provided shelter for these romantic encounters. Police reportedly did nothing to intervene when they found the self-appointed enforcers leveling the park's landscaping with hand-powered and motorized saws. Gays were outraged over what appeared to be the latest example of the anti-gay attitude of Lilly Law, not to mention homophobic citizens.

Vigilantes with chain saws. Bar raids. Bar closings. Police antagonism. How much more of this harassment was the gay community supposed to take? According to one chronicler of the scene, "On Wednesday and Thursday nights," following Pine's Tuesday raid, there was plenty of "grumbling." The observer noted, "Predominately, the theme was, 'This shit has got to stop!'"

Craig Rodwell would later assert that sometimes "everything comes together at one particular moment" and events turn into history. Think of Rosa Parks and the Montgomery bus boycott. Passengers had defied segregated seating on city buses before she refused to give up her seat on December 1, 1955, but it was the circumstances surrounding her defiance—from her activist standing in the community to the arrival of Martin Luther King, Jr., as the new young preacher in town—that fueled the successful boycott. Likewise, Seneca Falls, New York, wasn't the first place women thought to ask for their rights, and Selma, Alabama, wasn't the last place African Americans sought the right to vote, but both places became connected in history, along with the boycott in Montgomery, as revolutionary junctures in the American quest for civil rights.

Focusing on the present, Inspector Pine proceeded to plan his next Stonewall raid with his customary attention to detail. Pine had served commendably during World War II, both in the training of soldiers in hand-to-hand combat and as a veteran of front-line service. He wanted to make sure that his latest maneuver came off without incident. He assembled a small team to assist him and Detective Smythe with the raid. None of these police officers came from the Sixth Precinct, the unit responsible for the Stonewall's neighborhood. Pine didn't want an insider to tip off the bar about the planned raid. Instead he drafted four men from the public morals force to form the core of the raiding party, joined by two undercover policewomen from a neighboring precinct.

His plan was this: First, four undercover officers would enter the club, the two women and two of the four men from public morals. This party would mingle with patrons and observe the operation. Their eyewitness accounts would make it easier to sort out employees from customers after the raid began, and their reports could prove valuable during the prosecution of criminal behavior. These undercover observers were expected to survey the scene and leave. They would then cross Christopher Street, enter Christopher Park, and meet up with Pine, Smythe, and the other two officers from public morals. That party of eight, none of whom would be dressed in police uniforms, would then re-cross Christopher Street, knock on the bar's reinforced door, announce their police raid, and demand entry to the club.

Once inside, Pine's group would contact the Sixth Precinct for backup support using a portable two-way radio transmitter. Two additional authorities would join Pine's party to complete the group's reconnaissance. One was a member of the U.S. Bureau of Alcohol, Tobacco and Firearms; it was this man's job to evaluate the purity of the bar's liquor and determine whether the establishment was breaking any federal laws. The other investigator was a member of the city's consumer affairs department; he held the authority to comment on ways in which the bar failed to comply with city regulations, from sanitation to fire safety. This city code inspector would enter the bar with the undercover officers so he, too, could observe the business in operation.

Inspector Seymour Pine, New York Police Department, undated photo.

Pine intended to once again confiscate the Stonewall's supply of alcohol and to arrest the bar's employees. For good measure he would segregate cross-dressing patrons and arrest one as proof that the bar was admitting practitioners of this still-illegal form of expression. This time Pine planned to leave more lasting evidence of his presence, too. His visit on Tuesday had barely set back the bar at all; by Wednesday the Stonewall had reopened. Now Pine had obtained a court order that permitted him to remove key elements of the facility, including its jukeboxes and its bars, which he intended to have sawed into pieces and hauled away.

Pine held a pre-raid meeting with his seven-member team and the city code inspector near midnight on Friday, June 27. He wanted everyone on the same page of the playbook. Those gathered understood that the bar's cross-dressing customers would need to be isolated during the raid so that, if necessary, they could be privately examined to confirm that they were breaking the law. (Gender reassignment surgery had just begun that decade, so the female officers would be used to assure that none of the apparent cross-dressers really *was* a woman dressed up as a woman.) Faced with the prospect of an examination of their genitalia, most cross-dressers simply admitted their crime. Other customers would be allowed to depart after showing valid identification that they were of legal drinking age.

Gathered with his team at a police headquarters north of Greenwich Village, Pine recapped the details of his plan. First go undercover. Then regroup for the raid. Once inside, collar the employees, confiscate the booze, destroy the bar. Backup forces would help with the bar's destruction and the hauling away of prisoners. Pine's party would assure the evidence remained secure.

In, out, done. As simple as that.

CHAPTER 4

RAID!

"The police weren't letting us dance. If there's one place in the world where you can dance and feel yourself fully as a person and that's threatened with being taken away, those words are fighting words."

—TOMMY LANIGAN-SCHMIDT,
participant in the Stonewall riots

THE RAID BEGAN WITH A THUMP ON THE DOOR.

"Police! We're taking the place!" declared Seymour Pine as he rapped on the guarded entrance.

Anthony Verra, the Stonewall Inn's twenty-five-year-old doorman, and other security employees had no choice but to let the police enter. But even a few seconds' delay allowed someone to flash the lights and signal to those inside that the police had returned for another raid.

The hands of the clocks had cruised past midnight more than an hour before Pine's knock. Hundreds of revelers were packed into the Stonewall's two barrooms. They'd been drinking, and dancing, and, in some cases, consuming drugs for hours by then. It was something like 1:20 in the morning. A raid? Another raid? Now? Why? Am I going to be arrested? What's going on? Hundreds of heads clicked from party mode to panic mode with the flick of a light switch.

Protesters scuffle with police outside the Stonewall Inn during the pre-dawn hours of June 28, 1969.

"The place is under arrest," announced the police. Then the officers secured the Stonewall's door.

"I headed for the bathroom, hoping there was a window," Yvonne Ritter later recalled. "If there had been one I would've gone out of it." And for good reason. Ritter had begun exploring life as what would now be called a transgender person. Then known variously as Steve and Maria, on that night Maria was celebrating her eighteenth birthday while attired in one of her mother's party dresses, borrowed without her permission. Drinking at eighteen—legal. Wearing the clothing of the opposite gender— definitely against the law. Getting caught by your mother in one of her dresses—for Ritter, positively terrifying.

Authorities instructed patrons to line up, planning to check each person's identification to weed out lawbreakers. "It'll be over in a short time," an officer reassured the crowd.

One of the members of Pine's raiding party used a nearby pay phone to call the local police station. Only then did members of the Sixth Precinct learn that a bar in their jurisdiction was under assault. "Get your ass over to the Stonewall," the dispatcher advised the precinct's officers. Many of these law enforcers patrolled on foot and kept in touch with headquarters via a network of dedicated police call boxes located strategically throughout the city. "They're going to make a bust there," explained the precinct dispatcher. Uniformed officers arrived on foot, and some reinforcements from the precinct headquarters appeared in three patrol cars to join in the work of the raid.

Officers sorted the ensnared people into categories. Employees and cross-dressers were shunted to the back barroom in preparation for arrests. Other patrons moved toward the front bar for review and possible release. The go-go boys buried their gold bikini bottoms beneath street clothes, then joined the other employees in the back bar area. The undercover police helped identify other people they'd seen working as employees. The two female officers, who had not exited the bar prior to the raid, explained to Inspector Pine that they'd stayed inside to watch the work shift change from one set of employees to the next. Pine wondered if, in fact, they'd just become too caught up in playing the role of patrons. The city's code inspector had settled into his undercover job so completely that he'd failed to notice the figure he'd been chatting with at the time of the raid had been a man masquerading as a woman. Such minor details aside, as far as Pine could tell, everything was unfolding according to plan, and the raiding party began to confiscate the Stonewall's supply of alcohol.

"Together we stood vigil until they stopped letting our people out of the bar."

—MORTY MANFORD, recollecting the scene outside the Stonewall following his release during Pine's pre-dawn raid

Patrons waited nervously to be released, queuing up single file to pass through a checkpoint near the door. Some traded barbs with the police, resentful of the inspection process. Those lacking proper identification were detained for possible arrest; those with it were dismissed one by one out the door onto Christopher Street. If the bar had been sparsely populated that night, or if the raid had taken place a few years earlier, when such events represented a greater risk of arrest, people probably would have melted into the shadows with relief. But this night, most likely because so many people had been crowded into the bar, the released patrons began to congregate outside. They waited for friends. They waited to see if people they knew would be okay. They waited to see what would happen next.

Because it was a weekend night in a city known for its constant animation, the small crowd of exiting patrons triggered curiosity among the evening's passersby. Many of these pedestrians were gay, too. They saw friends, recognized the names of people they learned were inside, cared about the Stonewall. So they, too, stayed to watch. Tourists and other Village visitors and residents noticed the scene, and they hung around as well. Organically, the crowd began to grow. Soon more than a hundred people had congregated on the street and sidewalks outside the Stonewall Inn.

Pine, busy supervising the logistics of the raid, remained oblivious to the crowd forming outside. "Usually, when we went to work, everybody disappeared," Pine later recalled. "They were glad to get away."

But not this time.

This night the scene outside the Stonewall quickly morphed into a sort of improvisational street theater. With the building's façade serving as the perfect backdrop, the bar's door became the entry point onto a sidewalk stage, complete with a ready-made audience. The bar disgorged its customers one by one, and patrons so inclined began to camp it up for the waiting crowd. Individuals struck victory poses, arms thrown high in a celebratory V. They bowed to the crowd, as if appearing at a curtain call. They threw one-liners at nearby police officers—such as "Hello there, fella"—and blew kisses to onlookers. Members of the makeshift audience began to applaud, and the crowd continued to grow, both due to the release of bar patrons and from perpetual neighborhood foot traffic.

Craig Rodwell and his partner, Fred Sargeant, were returning home after a night of card playing with friends when they happened upon the Stonewall scene. "There was a feeling in the air that something was going to happen. This is different," Rodwell observed. They, too, stayed to watch. "Things started off small,"

Sargeant later recalled, "but there was an energy that began to flow through the crowd."

A police paddy wagon arrived, signaling that arrests were going to be made. This vehicle looked a bit like a cross between a panel van and a package delivery truck. The cargo hold had windowless sides and was accessed through a rear-loading door. Fixed benches lined the interior to hold its ill-fated passengers. The boisterous crowd outside the Stonewall became subdued at the sight of the vehicle. Were any of their friends bound for jail? Rumors swirled about beatings underway inside the bar. Were people being attacked by Lilly Law? Plus, what about the Stonewall itself? Some departing customers had watched the authorities start to destroy the interior furnishings. What was going on in there? What would happen next on the street?

Pine ordered the Stonewall's employees to be loaded first into the waiting paddy wagon. The crowd blew raspberries of disapproval at the Mafia managers, but they responded more sympathetically as they watched ordinary employees walk toward the van, including the attendant who stocked the restrooms. Some people applauded and cheered.

Rodwell, who stood with Sargeant somewhat above the crowd, having perched on the landing of a neighboring building entrance, recognized the raid as a reason for gay activism. Improvising on the "Black power" slogan of the increasingly militant civil rights movement, he shouted a parallel rallying cry at the crowd below: "Gay power!" It was a cry for change, a call to action. A few others echoed his idea of protest by singing the civil rights anthem "We Shall Overcome," but neither gesture took off. The crowd was more transfixed by unfolding developments than by their political implications.

Inside the Stonewall, out of sight from the street scene, Pine found his team tangling with such resistance among the cross-dressers that he abandoned his plan of arresting only a token representative of this law-breaking group. Instead he ordered them all detained. The dramatic appearances these individuals made as they greeted the waiting crowd resulted in laughter, admiration, and growing anger.

The crowd's mood darkened considerably when it became clear that all of the cross-dressers were being arrested. Some cooperated with their detention, but others did not. Tension grew on both sides, with the police becoming increasingly rough and those under arrest becoming more and more quarrelsome. A few prisoners managed to escape in the chaos of the night, including a key pair of Stonewall employees. Sixth Precinct officers may well have deliberately allowed the men to get away in order to keep cozy with the bar's Mafia owners. Even the youth who had arrived at the Stonewall as Maria Ritter—eager to avoid a mother's wrath over that borrowed party dress—managed to find a sympathetic police officer and slipped out of the paddy wagon.

"There is a limit, and Friday night was it."

—RONNIE DI BRIENZA, explaining the mob reaction
to Pine's second raid of the Stonewall Inn

By this time Inspector Pine knew his raid had problems. Freed patrons and others had formed into a crowd. The detained cross-dressers were giving him grief. He now had more prisoners to transport to headquarters than would fit in a single police van, and he lacked the manpower required to manage the increasingly complex and unstable scene. Furthermore, he was having trouble communicating his situation to the nearby precinct because his radio operator couldn't manage to connect to the dispatch center.

And then there were the lesbians.

Differences of fact and opinion swirl around that night's scene in general and certain details in particular—especially when it comes to the role that lesbians played during the raid. Such controversies are not uncommon in history, and it makes sense that they occur. When people watch an athletic contest, they witness a relatively orderly event, and generally there is agreement about the facts of the game. Who scored. Who won. Even which team played better. Disputes are relatively rare. Referees who represent various vantage points help to settle them, and multiple cameras document the action.

But if, for example, a fight breaks out on a playground, the facts may need to be reconstructed from the reports of participants and witnesses. Details often remain in dispute depending on how physically close someone was to the conflict, the level of chaos at the center of the disagreement, rumors about conflicting details, and alliances people have to the opposing sides. Further complicating the narrative are people who claim to know more than they really do because they want to assert their proximity to the scene. Even eyewitnesses who speak authentically can only attest to their personal, two-eyed view of the action. In short, no one can take in every detail, especially when an event involves so many sub-components of simultaneous activity. Such was the case at the Stonewall on that hot night in 1969.

Although the vast majority of the Stonewall's patrons that evening were men, just as on other occasions, some women had been ensnared in the raid, too. Most of these individuals, like the men, preferred same-sex partners. These patrons, as well as others influenced by the era's women's liberation movement, could easily have found themselves lacking the three officially prescribed gender-appropriate articles of clothing because by then some women had eliminated bras from their wardrobes. This meant the bar's female patrons were more likely to be arrested than were gay men, only a few of whom stood out as cross-dressers.

Women faced a disadvantage, too, during an era when virtually all police officers were male. This fact trapped them in the same male-dominated dynamic that helped fuel the women's movement: the man held the power, and the woman was expected to submit to his authority. Lesbians bore the likelihood of triggering an extra dose of scorn, at best, and abuse, at worst, from disapproving male officers.

Inevitable tensions built that night at the Stonewall as the police manhandled the lesbians caught up in the raid. Officers groped at least some of them and treated them discourteously. Witnesses claim that a lesbian in masculine attire protested the rough handling and received, in response, a billy club blow to the head. By that time, if not before, she had been pushed facedown on the floor, forced into handcuffs with her hands behind her back, and placed under arrest.

Having filled the paddy wagon with Mafia men, bar employees, and some of the cross-dressing patrons, the police began loading other prisoners into the three available squad cars. At this time someone, perhaps the handcuffed lesbian, or perhaps another one, or perhaps even a gender-ambiguous male, exited the Stonewall under police escort in a decidedly combative mood. The person had been harassed, attacked, and handcuffed, all for showing up at a gay bar. Members of the crowd stood riveted as this individual fought being marched to a police car, refused to stay put in the car, and repeatedly exited it until, after the final escape attempt, the person was literally lifted off the ground by an officer and thrown forcibly into the vehicle. This skirmish lasted several minutes or more.

Not everyone saw or remembered the scuffle—a testament to how chaotic the street scene had become—but almost all of the people who did see it perceived this person to be a lesbian in men's clothing. The woman's struggle with the police was shocking. Some recall her turning to the street crowd at one point and exclaiming, "Why don't you guys do something?!"

That did it.

The tension of that night and countless previous nights and hundreds of lifetimes of abuse burst the dams of person after person. The crowd became a mob, and the mob began to riot. People began shouting obscenities at the police. They started throwing copper pennies at them in a sign of disrespect: Copper coins for the cops. Copper coins for the coppers. "Dirty copper!" people yelled as they flicked pennies at the police. "Let's pay them off," others shouted, in a reference to the payoffs made to the authorities by the Mafia.

Nickels followed pennies. Quarters followed nickels. A hail of change rained down on the police. It rang a discordant tune as it bounced off police cars, clattered against the walls and windows of the Stonewall, and struck members of the force. Gone were the songs of peaceful protest. This tune sounded the call to revolution.

Reports of the raid had already been spreading by word of mouth through the gay community. Eyewitnesses ran through the streets like modern-day Paul Reveres to shout the news. Others dashed to the area's plentiful pay phones, slipped dimes into the machines, and told their friends: get down here. As Stonewall historian David Carter writes, "Word of the

A New York Police Department complaint form related to the June 28, 1969 unrest outside of the Stonewall Inn.

raid passed through the night like a fever," and the rioting mob grew larger.

A shower of empty glass bottles joined the downpour of coins. Beer bottles. Wine bottles. Glass soft drink bottles. Any bottle that people could grab, aim, and throw. Someone pried a cobblestone out of the ground and lobbed it with a crash onto the trunk of one of the squad cars. The ever-swelling crowd advanced toward the officers and began banging on the paddy wagon, pounding on the windows and doors of the squad cars, pushing and bouncing the vehicles until they rocked unsteadily on their wheels. Witnesses report that at least some of the police cars' tires were slashed with a knife, crippling the vehicles.

Rioters began to surge like waves of surf, moving toward and away from the Stonewall, advancing as close as they dared, then retreating to stay clear of the reach of billy clubs. Members of the pulsing, swelling crowd discovered a stash of bricks at a nearby construction site. Soon bricks, too, were flying through the air toward the police.

Having filled the paddy wagon and the three squad cars to capacity with prisoners, Inspector Pine instructed escorting officers to "just drop [the prisoners] at the Sixth Precinct and hurry back." The vehicles only needed to travel a short distance, not even a dozen blocks. So close, and yet so far away. Pine still could not make contact with the station to request additional support. "Hurry back," he said.

The departure of this convoy left Pine standing outside the Stonewall with, essentially, his original raiding party as support: Detective Smythe, the four undercover officers, and the other two members of the public morals team. A uniformed patrolman from the Sixth Precinct named Gil Weissman and the city code inspector remained behind with them, too. This small force needed to secure the Stonewall Inn as a crime scene, conclude the gathering of evidence, and transport the remaining prisoners to headquarters.

Plus there was that mob to deal with.

The crowd gave Pine little time to reflect on what to do next. He had served in World War II, and he understood the gravity of his situation. "We didn't have the manpower, and the manpower for the other side was coming like it was a real war. And that's what it was, it was a war." As one counterculture journalist wrote after witnessing the scene: "You could see the fear and disbelief on the faces of the pigs." The authorities may have been better armed—they did possess guns, after all—but they were overwhelmingly outnumbered, at least until reinforcements arrived. If this was a war, the military maneuver that best suited their situation was obvious.

Retreat.

Civil rights protests. Anti-war protests. Political protests. Race riots. Everyone knew the drill. Protesters got so far, and then the police triumphed. With billy clubs. With tear gas. With over-whelming force. But not this night. This night was different.

This night the cops were on the run.

CHAPTER 5

REVOLUTION

> *"You could hear screaming outside, a lot of noise from the protesters, and it was a good sound. It was a real good sound to know that, you know, you had a lot of people out there pulling for you."* —RAYMOND CASTRO,
> a Stonewall Inn patron being detained
> inside the bar during its siege

"IT WAS TERRIFYING," SEYMOUR PINE LATER ADMITTED. THE decorated veteran described the riots outside the Stonewall Inn as being "as bad as any situation that I had met in during the army." After the departure of the prisoner convoy, the space separating Pine's small force from the seething mob of bottle-throwing adversaries melted away. *Village Voice* reporter Howard Smith, who had begun to shadow Inspector Pine after happening upon the unrest, estimated that no more than ten feet separated the two sides.

"Let's go inside," Pine suggested to his colleagues. "Lock ourselves inside; it's safer." Pine expected reinforcements to return in a matter of minutes and reasoned that his team would be secure on the other side of the Stonewall Inn's reinforced door during this brief wait. He turned to the nearby *Village Voice* reporter and asked, "You want to come in?"

Smith considered his options. He had spotted the raid's gathering crowd early on from his nearby newspaper office and had rushed to cover the developing scene. By following Inspector Pine he had been

The Stonewall Inn, 51–53 Christopher Street, July 2, 1969.

able to observe the operations of the raid. Now what should he do? His long-haired appearance fit his role as a reporter for the trendy *Voice* and gave him street credibility among the younger members of the mob. But the press pass hanging from his neck and the company he'd been keeping with police officers might mislead rioters into thinking he worked for the authorities instead of a newspaper. Smith weighed the journalistic downside of leaving the street action versus his risk of being beaten by the mob if he remained. Maybe he could learn something by hanging out further with the police, he reasoned. "In goes me," Smith decided.

Pine, his accompanying party of eight law enforcement officials, the city code inspector, and the *Voice* reporter retreated into the Stonewall Inn. Then they bolted the bar's door behind them, converting the defenses that had been meant to deter the police into tools for their own protection. This maneuver had the unintended consequence of further enraging the mob. "That's when it really started in earnest and spread," Craig Rodwell recalled. Now the police weren't just busting the Stonewall; they were occupying it. The audacity of the act—a combination of denial and desecration—not only infuriated the crowd; it gave them a purpose: take back the Stonewall.

Those in Pine's party, locked inside the bar behind its wood and steel double door and wood-covered windows, could no longer see the exterior action. Sound became the best source for conjecture about the scene outside. The torrent of thuds hitting the walls and windows of the bar suggested that a hail of bricks and cobblestones had punctuated their retreat into the building, which was indeed the case. A persistent cacophony of thumps and the shattering of glass blended with the howl of the mob, its general roar of disapproval marked by periodic shouts of intelligible speech. "Pigs!" "Gay power!" "Occupy—take over, take over." Exclamations and cheers followed particularly well-aimed strikes.

A number of other people found themselves trapped inside the assaulted space as unintentional companions of the police team and its shadowing reporter. The Stonewall's bartender. Cross-dressers. Additional arrested patrons, left behind after the first haul of prisoners had departed the area. They, too, listened to the bellowing, belligerent crowd, amazed, perhaps, by the reaction triggered by their predicament.

Lucian Truscott IV, another reporter for the *Village Voice*, had happened upon the Stonewall raid just like Smith. The two news-men had crossed paths briefly soon after the raid began and then had become separated. By accident they managed to position themselves to strategic advantage, with Smith inside the Stonewall and Truscott remaining street-side, balanced on top of an upended garbage can to enhance his view of the scene.

"Our goal was to hurt those police," explained John O'Brien, a gay man and activist who had joined the mob. "I wanted to kill those cops for the anger I had in me. And the cops got that. And they were lucky that door was closed, they were very lucky." Doric Wilson, another riot participant, observed, "There was joy because the cops weren't winning. The cops were barricaded inside. We were winning." Another activist, this one a devotee to the non-violent philosophy of the times, found himself wrestling with an internal dilemma after the violence broke out. Should he partici-pate or not? "Ah, what the hell! Yeah!" Kevin Dunn decided. "And then I started scrambling to pick up whatever I could find" that could be added to the rain of debris.

The crowd of catcalling, coin-tossing bystanders became an assaulting army with a corresponding escalation and variety in its choice of missiles. Drink cans joined bottles. Refuse material-ized from city trash baskets. Then came the baskets themselves. Someone even tried to seize Truscott's own trash-can perch.

And then there was the parking meter.

To Smith and the others inside, it seemed as if rioters were only systematically pelting the door with cobblestones. Those witnesses who shared Truscott's point of view knew otherwise. An unlikely team of effeminate and muscular gays had managed to uproot a nearby parking meter and convert it into a battering ram. *Bam. Bam. Bam.* They butted the heavy metal head of the meter against the Stonewall's double-thick door. Smith, Pine, and the other nearby officers felt the building shake with the unknown objects' impact and watched as the door began to weaken from the blows.

Bam, bam, BAM! The door gave way. Before the police could re-secure the entrance, rioters propelled a cascade of projectiles through the opening. Beer bottles. Beer cans. Other trash. More coins. "The cops inside were scared shitless, dodging projectiles and flying glass," recounted one of the street-side witnesses to the scene.

The ensuing confusion of contradictory accounts suggests that it may have been at this point that a flying object injured Officer Gil Weissman. Stonewall historian David Carter, based on his analysis of conflicting sources, discounts the reliability of Smith's description and places this incident prior to the siege of the Stonewall. But, if Smith's account is accepted as reliable—and he was taking notes through most of the riot—then the opposite conclusion is possible. Smith later reported in the *Village Voice,*

> The door crashes open, beer cans and bottles hurtle in. Pine and his troop rush to shut it. At that point the only uniformed cop among them gets hit with something under his eye. He hollers, and his hand comes away scarlet. It looks a lot more serious than it really is. They are all suddenly furious. Three run out in front to see if they can scare the mob from the door. A hail of coins. A beer can glances off Deputy Inspector Smythe's head.
>
> Pine . . . leaps out into the melee, and grabs someone around the waist, pulling him downward and back into the doorway. They fall. Pine regains hold and drags the elected protester inside by his hair. The door slams again.

Pine's captive was a tall, bearded folk musician named Dave Van Ronk, a straight spectator who had been dining at a neighboring restaurant and come out to investigate (and then joined) the street commotion. Pine had needed help securing the six-foot-five-inch-tall Van Ronk, in part because members of the crowd tried to tug him back to safety during their scuffle. After pulling Van Ronk inside, the officers completed their arrest by slapping and punching him in the face and kicking his prone figure. Then they capped off just the sort of behavior that infuriated such people as that night's rioters by handcuffing the nearly unconscious man to a radiator near the doorway.

Dave Van Ronk, performing at the Gaslight coffee house in Greenwich Village, November 8, 1963.

Being able to reclose the Stonewall's door—even with the apprehension at that time of one member of the crowd—offered small consolation to those trapped inside. What was the likelihood that the door would stay shut? And what about all those other angry people on the other side? What would happen if they came tumbling through the door or windows?

Most of all, where were the reinforcements? More than enough minutes had elapsed for that original convoy to have reached the precinct office and returned to the Stonewall, and yet no further help had materialized. No explanations have ever fully accounted for this delay, but one plausible idea is that precinct regulars, on the take from the Mafia, felt no urgency to rush back and assist a unit that had busted one of its neighborhood establishments without warning. Those still at the Stonewall were left to wonder how best to hold on.

Officers began piling furniture in front of the door and windows as further reinforcement against intruders. They scoured the interior of the bar for other weapons. One man found a sawed-off baseball bat. The *Voice* reporter unearthed a heavy tool—some say a wrench, others a fire axe—and tucked it into his belt. Even so, the continual assault on the bar's windows began to have an effect. The exterior glass panes closest to the street were long gone, and the interior layer of plywood, even with its crossbar reinforcement of a two-by-four, began to fracture. Small peepholes developed, offering those inside a chance to again see their adversaries. "We were shocked," Smith later commented, "at how big the crowd had become." Plus, he noted, "they were getting more ferocious."

Jerry Hoose had been summoned to the scene by a phone call from a friend. "I'd been waiting for this to happen," he later recalled. "I knew it was going to happen. I said, 'Great!' I was the happiest person on the face of the earth; I'm sure I had tears of joy. And I was willing to do anything. I wanted to get into it. Everybody was angry. We were angry people, and we had a lot of reason to be angry."

The throngs on the street were in no way deterred by the reclosing of the Stonewall's door. They simply redoubled their efforts to breach the entrance and attack the police inside. "The orgy was taking place," observed one sympathetic witness whose account of the riots was published under the headline, "Queen Power: Fags Against Pigs in Stonewall Bust." The writer continued, explaining the motivations for the rioting: "Vengeance vented against the source of repression—gay bars, busts, kids victimized and exploited by the Mafia and cops." The correspondent added, "Strangely, no one spoke to the crowd or tried to direct the insurrection. Everyone's heads were in the same place."

Activists took part in the attack, as did some cross-dressers and other gays. But the so-called queens of the era—effeminate men, many still teenaged, who affected feminine mannerisms but didn't necessarily cross-dress—drove the show, all united in a shared fight against their oppression. Mattachine activist and riot participant Dick Leitsch authored an account of the riots that noted, "It was the queens who scored the points and proved that they were not going to tolerate any more harassment or abuse."

Working individually and in small groups, members of the crowd added a new weapon to their arsenal: fire. Some created makeshift firebombs using soft drink bottles and flammable liquids such as cigarette lighter fluid. All they had to do was add a fuse, light, and toss. Others crammed wads of paper into the crevasses that had appeared in the bar's west window frame, doused them in lighter fluid, and set them afire. Still others lodged a wire-cage trash basket in the weakened window barricade and ignited its contents. Being trapped in a burning building became one more concern for Pine and his companions.

The officers had discovered a fire extinguisher in the course of their interior prowls, as well as a modest fire hose. They had previously employed the hose in an attempt to force attackers back from the face of the building, but instead the gentle spray of water had merely entertained—and probably provided cooling relief to—an active crowd on a still-hot night. Now the police trained the hose on the burning trash, having quickly exhausted the fire extinguisher's contents. Even this use of the hose was a mere half measure, since water will not extinguish a fuel-based fire.

With no police in sight, the mob—now numbering as many as two thousand—continued to shout and demonstrate outside the Stonewall Inn, simultaneously attacking both its door and its west window. Those inside had passed as many as thirty minutes under siege by this point, time ticking by to the tune of the methodical thudding of cobblestones, bricks, and a parking meter on the building's exterior. Residents from upper-story apartments around Christopher Park, growing tired of the neighborhood disruption, added their complaints to the night air and began tossing bottles out of their windows onto the rioters below. Yet still no backup support arrived to disperse the mob.

"I was sure we were gonna be killed."

—HOWARD SMITH, reporter for the *Village Voice*,
recollecting the siege of the Stonewall Inn

Despite repeated attempts, the on-site law enforcement team had been unable to contact the Sixth Precinct headquarters to find out why no one came to its aid. Neither its portable police radio transmitter nor the bar's telephone would connect. With growing concern, Pine's team began reinvestigating the Stonewall premises for other avenues of escape. Having determined at the beginning of the raid that the bar had no back windows, the group now discovered a small ceiling vent that led to the building's roof. With difficulty, the smallest police officer—one of the two undercover females—was able to squeeze through the vent and escape the scene. Pine instructed her to avoid Christopher Street and head for a nearby fire station. She could sound a fire alarm there plus telephone for further police assistance.

Once again the marooned officers began to mark time—how long might it take for word of their condition to be heard and addressed? But by this point their guns were drawn. Near the beginning of the assault, Howard Smith had asked members of the police force, "Aren't you guys scared?" Despite their assurances to the contrary, Smith thought they looked "at least uneasy." Now there was no question about it. Everyone was afraid.

Fires continued to sprout at the Stonewall's door and west window. The front door, having been repeatedly forced open, stood ajar though guarded as projectiles crossed its threshold. At least some of the rioters could see and hear the police threatening them with drawn weapons at the door and west window. "The kids were really scared about going too far," noted one street-side witness, and they kept an edgy distance from the bar.

Now Pine's biggest concern became the potential for gunfire. Admittedly the police found themselves in a grave situation, but even in the midst of the crisis Pine recognized that gunfire was a disproportional response for the crime he had been sent to address. "You knew that the first shot that was fired meant all the shots would be fired," Pine later explained, and yet even with gunfire the police unit would inevitably have been overrun, possibly killed.

Pine walked from officer to officer, addressing each one individually using a technique that had proven effective for him during the Second World War. By touching each person's shoulder or arm and engaging them in a brief status check, he dispelled some of the accumulated anxiety. As an added measure, he warned the officers that he would banish them to the city borough of "Staten Island all alone on a lonely beach for the rest of your police career" if they fired without his order.

"Nobody fire! Nobody fire!" Pine commanded. "Let's back up if we have to. Help's going to be coming."

Shattering glass, the roar of two thousand voices, sporadic calls for vengeance—all blended into the cacophony of a revolution. And then one more sound added its force to the night's tune. In the neighborhood. On the street. Within the battered walls of the Stonewall Inn. Everyone heard the noise.

At last.

The sound of relief. The sound of trouble.

Sirens.

CHAPTER 6

STREET WARS

"In the civil rights movement, we ran from the police, in the peace movement, we ran from the police. That night, the police ran from us, the lowliest of the low. And it was fantastic."

—JOHN O'BRIEN,

participant in the Stonewall riots, recalling the scene on June 28, 1969

SIRENS.

Thousands of minds processed the sound in an instant. For news reporter Howard Smith and his police companions, the wailing cry meant safety. "When I heard the sirens, I was pretty damn happy," he noted. According to the reporter, the brief refuge sought by the police inside the Stonewall had stretched on for an interminable forty-five minutes. Now their wait was surely over.

For the mob on the street, the sound of sirens signaled potential disaster, and the obvious response was simple: run! Like a just-broken rack of billiard balls, rioters dispersed scattershot around the Christopher Park area. But they didn't wholly desert the scene. This crowd had gained too much power and retained too much

Young people congregate outside the Stonewall Inn the evening of June 28, 1969, less than twenty-four hours after protesters had clashed with police during the pre-dawn raid.

fury to simply vanish. If the first act of the evening's engagement had been the stage show in front of the Stonewall, and act two had been its siege, act three became a choreographed street dance between protesters and police.

"There were more people out there when I came out than when I went in. Things were still flying through the air, cacophony—I mean just screaming and yelling, sirens, strobe lights, the whole spaghetti."

—DAVE VAN RONK, upon emerging
from the Stonewall Inn following its siege

About thirty officers from nearby precincts arrived in the latest convoy of assistance, accompanied by fire-fighting equipment and a paddy wagon. This small force was still vastly outnumbered, but the shock value of its arrival served initially to mute the intensity of the riot. Inspector Pine, after confirming the safety of reentering the street, began to methodically complete the steps of his raid. Survey the damage. Load the remaining prisoners. Secure the confiscated alcohol. Yet even these procedures proved difficult. Some of the arrested patrons resisted being loaded into the paddy wagon, and onlookers added to the chaos by renewing their campaign of shouting and bottle throwing. The police scuffled with rioters, triggering arrests that further provoked the crowd. Even the employment of high-pressure fire hoses failed to disperse the mob.

"Riot pigs," someone had shouted at the onset of the recent chorus of sirens. This contempt-filled phrase referenced not the regular

Members of the Tactical Patrol Force practice mob control during training exercises at the New York Police Academy gym, circa July 1968. The next year officers from this force tangled with protesters during the Stonewall riots.

precinct officers but the city's riot police—otherwise known as the Tactical Patrol Force, or TPF. Small details of this elite corps of police officers added their weight to the work of neighborhood squads in high-crime parts of New York City. Alternatively, hundreds of them could be rounded up on short notice to respond to major outbreaks of unrest. Reports of the deteriorating scene outside the Stonewall had triggered a TPF alert, and soon that riot-pig warning cry was validated by the arrival of busloads of officers. "These guys had helmets and lived to break heads," observed riot eyewitness Bob Kohler.

When the mere appearance of this manpower failed to empty the streets, groups of officers assumed their traditional wedge-shaped formations and began to sweep the city blocks. Standing shoulder to shoulder, eyes front, shields protecting their torsos, and with reinforcements marching behind, their lines filled the width of a street. The TPF had employed this maneuver with success countless times. The steps were simple. Don't go too fast. Hold firm. Never waver. Activists such as John O'Brien, a veteran of other protests, knew the drill. The mere threat of being clubbed by this phalanx of advancing nightsticks tended to convince anyone in its path to yield ground. And so it did during the early morning hours of June 28, 1969.

Sort of.

TPF maneuvers had been designed to control crowds within the orderly grid of Manhattan city blocks that unfolded north of Fourteenth Street. But the helter-skelter web of West Village streets didn't fit that mold. TPF officers bused in for service from other parts of the city were unfamiliar with the crazy-quilt pattern of the Stonewall's neighborhood. Rioters quickly figured out that all they had to do to outsmart the TPF was to run away from the advancing line, dash around three short blocks, and come up behind the force that had just watched them disappear from view. Instead of sweeping the streets, the TPF found itself ricocheting from one end of a block to the other, retracing steps without reducing the disorder.

The West Village was home turf for many members of the mob, and gays were tired of having their neighborhood invaded by outside authorities. "We were like a Hydra," Martin Boyce observed. "You cut one head off. For the first time the next person stood up." Participant Charles Burch recalled, "Years and years of all the resentments and humiliations and things that can come down on the head of a gay person were really—I was really experiencing liberation and radicalization and everything—*bang!*, right then and there."

This newest wave of protest generated a fresh soundtrack. Pounding feet. Shouts of direction. Chants of exclamation from participants, including Craig Rodwell's cries of "Gay power! Gay power!" Plus the continuing crash of broken glass as a seemingly endless supply of bottles became weapons to lob at the police. Rioters not engaged in games of chase contributed to the general chaos of the night by yelling at the pursuers, adding to the rain of debris, and kindling fires in city trash baskets.

"You didn't want to get hit by nightsticks.
Yet I had to see what was happening.
I had to see! This was unbelievable. My God!"

—DANNY GARVIN, a participant in the riots
following Pine's weekend Stonewall raid

As if the TPF wasn't already frustrated enough in its effort to stop the street action, some of the gay youths found an additional way to mock the elite force. When one group of officers approached Boyce and his friends, something about that solid line of men in matching uniforms, moving forward in unison, triggered a collective light bulb in the minds of the young gays. The streetwise participants, mimicking the police formation, locked arms, lifted alternating legs in a chorus-line-worthy kick, and began to sing: "We are the Village Girls. / We wear our hair in curls . . ."

The TPF had never seen anything like it. Nothing in its training or experience had prepared the officers for such a response. They knew how to stay in formation when confronting a wall of antiwar passive resistance, advancing toward the immobile crowd and penetrating the grid of resistance. They knew how to stay in formation when confronting walls of violence, advancing step by matching step even as bottles and rocks bounced off of their shields and helmets. But a Broadway kick line? Never! Absent any better plan, the blue-uniformed TPF continued to advance as the teens maintained their show of defiant glee.

"We wear our dungarees / above our nelly knees," the youths sang. They taunted the police with nicknames. Lilly Law. The girls in blue. Then, when just out of arm's reach, the savvy street kids bolted.

Mocked. Teased. Outwitted. Once again the police had been outmaneuvered by the protesters. That night inventive gays led the TPF on endless pursuits through the tangled knot of darkened Village streets. Boyce recalled at least one occasion when the police changed their strategy and charged the taunting teens. "They got me in the back with a stick," he reported ruefully. Other blows landed on the heads of rioters, and even bystanders, as the skirmishes continued for an hour or more.

The evening's events had left the regular police officers "totally humiliated," observed riot witness Kohler. "Everybody in America who had a beef had already rioted, but the fairies were not supposed to riot. And nobody else had ever won," Kohler explained. "No other group had ever forced cops to retreat before, so the anger was just enormous" among the TPF officers. Revenge fueled their actions, Kohler implied, adding, "I mean, they wanted to kill."

Amazingly, no one died during the night's riot, or was even critically hurt. A handful of police officers, including Gil Weissman, reported injuries. No tallies were recorded of wounded civilians. The arrest log for the extended disorder yielded barely a dozen names, and none of those people received significant punishment. Pine's team had carted away not even twenty bottles of alcohol and fewer than thirty cases of beer. Perhaps the biggest casualty of the evening was the Stonewall itself. *Village Voice* reporter Truscott visited the bar at the conclusion of the raid. According to him, the police "took bats and just busted that place up. The mirrors, all the bottles of liquor, the jukebox, the cigarette machines." Add the destructive force of rioters during the siege, and the bar's demise looked complete.

The night's unrest wound down of its own accord after fatigue, satisfaction, and even boredom overtook the fragmented forces of the mob. Not until after 4 a.m., some three hours since Inspector Pine's knock on the Stonewall Inn's door, did calm and order begin to return to the streets. Having bested the cops not just once with the siege but again during the street chases, rioters began to slip away, or turn into spectators, or adjourn to nearby residential stoops where they could marvel over the unexpected outcome for what should have been an ordinary police raid.

In, out, done. As simple as that, the police had thought.

But not this time.

CHAPTER 7

THE AWAKENING

> "I thought, my God, we're going to pay so desperately for this, there was glass all over. But the next day we didn't pay. My father called and congratulated me. He said, 'What took you so long?'"
>
> —MARTIN BOYCE,
> recollecting the morning
> after the Stonewall riots

REMARKABLY, THE DAY THAT FOLLOWED THE STONEWALL riots did not mark the end for the Stonewall Inn. Before dark that Saturday night, it had already reopened, albeit without the service of alcohol. Nor did the light of day dampen the sentiments that had been stirred up by the riots of the previous evening. Individuals who had witnessed or participated in the unrest began spreading the word to those who had missed it. Many locals who heard the news traveled to the West Village so they could see the destruction for themselves. Trash bins with charred refuse and sparkling glass shards confirmed the scope of the previous night's rage.

Two themes quickly emerged within the gay community. Older and more traditional figures were generally unsettled by news of the public protests. These individuals tended to be more

Young gays gather on the steps of a Christopher Street building near the Stonewall Inn the evening after the bar's pre-dawn raid.

closeted and risked losing their jobs and livelihoods if their sexual orientations were disclosed. Plus, older gays had for decades been reminded by straight society that same-sex attraction was a mental illness, something to wrestle with and hide, not something worthy of pride and respect. Rioting in the streets? Challenging the police? Blatant displays of queen-inspired camp? The whole idea was beyond shocking.

Younger gays and participants in the Stonewall riot felt shocked, too, but at the other end of the spectrum. Overnight they went from being isolated, angry individuals to becoming members of the same extended family. These gays realized, "Oh my God. I am not alone. There are other people that feel exactly the same way," explained Doric Wilson. "We became a people," observed Danny Garvin. "All of a sudden, I had brothers and sisters." What was more, members of this newfound community had tasted freedom and equality. After Friday night's quest for liberation and self-expression, there was no turning back. Even the police and other straights were having epiphanies. "People are beginning to realize," the doorman of the Stonewall Inn observed a few days after the riot, "that no matter how 'nelly' or how 'fem' a homosexual is, you can only push them so far."

Craig Rodwell had been waiting for years for the spark that would ignite a widespread gay rights movement, and he recognized immediately that the riots on Christopher Street could be that catalyst. Rodwell, working with his partner Fred Sargeant, seized the day. "We knew that this was a moment that we didn't want to let slip past." All those years of organizing and protest meant that Rodwell knew exactly what he needed to capitalize on the energy of the moment. He needed a leaflet.

Before the era of Facebook and Twitter and before the photocopy machine was common, the best way to spread news quickly was by publishing a leaflet. Rodwell titled his "Get the Mafia and the Cops out of Gay Bars." He wrote it immediately after the riot, and, by Saturday afternoon, he and Sargeant had had five thousand copies commercially printed. That same day the two recruited gender-balanced pairs of gay men and lesbians to help distribute the statement, using a strategy Rodwell had employed successfully for years through his youth group HYMN.

Rodwell's leaflet predicted that the previous night's uprising "will go down in history as the first time that thousands of homosexual men and women went out into the streets to protest the intolerable situation which has existed in New York City for many years." It called on that same community to act again, with gays opening their own bars, boycotting corrupt places such as the Stonewall, and appealing to the city mayor for greater law-enforcement accountability.

Dick Leitsch, president of the Mattachine Society of New York and riot witness, created an instant leaflet, too. He called his "The Hairpin Drop Heard Around the World," combining references to the first Revolutionary War shots of Lexington and Concord with the gay slang expression for revealing one's homosexuality.

A message from the Mattachine Society of New York painted on the boarded-up windows of the Stonewall Inn, June 28, 1969. Some members of the gay community called for calm following the riots. Others urged revolution.

Leitsch's leaflet recounted his eyewitness view of the riots and joined Rodwell's that weekend on the streets of New York.

The management of the Stonewall Inn—always eager to keep the money flowing in—tried to lure back its customers Saturday evening with an improvised sound system and free soft drinks. Gone was the gatekeeping, the log book, the secrecy. And, with the service of alcohol dropped, gone was the excuse for further police raids. "We run a legitimate joint here. There ain't nuttin' bein' done wrong in dis place," the *Voice*'s Lucian Truscott reported the staff as saying, with ethnic accents and all. "Everybody come and see."

"I was very angry, and it's funny, the immediate gay consciousness that happened to me."

—KEVIN BREW, recollecting the impact of the Stonewall riots

A few patrons ventured inside, but more people gathered outside on the summer evening. People from the gay community and beyond wanted to visit the battlefront, as it were, and to be on hand if further action developed. A heavy police presence—intended to discourage renewed violence—instead inflamed the tensions of the previous night. Officers welcomed the chance to exercise their authority. Crowd members resented this repeat invasion of their home turf and chafed at being ordered to stay in motion. No stationary groups. No large gatherings. It felt like a return to past treatments, as in, "Keep moving, faggot, keep moving."

A day of record-setting, ninety-five-degree heat just added to overall irritability. As night fell, the numbers of people milling about on the streets rose from the hundreds to the thousands. Early-evening cheers of "Gay power" and exhibitions of same-sex hand-holding and kissing inevitably gave way to grumbling. Street youths reprised their kick-line performance of the previous night, daring police to attack them as they sang additional verses of their ditty:

> *We are the Stonewall girls.*
> *We wear our hair in curls.*
> *We have no underwear.*
> *We show our pubic hairs.*

Members of the crowd seized on the idea of taking control of Christopher Street. If they couldn't have equality everywhere, they could at least demonstrate for it on this one significant stretch of territory. If heterosexuals experienced inconvenience, discomfort, and discrimination, oh well, they reasoned, welcome to our world. A new round of chants sprang up: "Liberate the street!" "Christopher Street belongs to the queens!" Protesters moved into the street, blocked traffic, and rocked vehicles back and forth.

Such misbehavior inevitably triggered calls by local police for reinforcements, and the TPF arrived to engage with protesters in what became a repeat of the previous night's street choreography. Once again savvy activists led the force on fruitless chases, doubling back around to taunt their pursuers. Once again gay youths made stands with their kick lines. And, once again, violence broke out on both sides. Bottles were thrown. Billy clubs swung. Fires were set. Head wounds drew blood. The police added tear gas to the mix. Rioters converted metal garbage can lids into oversized Frisbees. On one occasion, a sizeable group of participants reversed course and charged an unusually small contingent of officers who had been pursuing them. "Catch them!" people shouted, threatening, presumably in jest, to rape the cops if they did. (Neither event occurred.)

Bedlam continued for hours. Eventually the TPF did manage to secure the block of Christopher Street in front of the Stonewall, but that accomplishment mainly served to assure that patrons couldn't reach other restaurants and bars along the popular corridor. Skirmishes and dustups continued until two or three the next morning. Leitsch later joked that protesters eventually left the streets to hang out at the dockside trucks. With the police congregated around the Stonewall, gays could gather undisturbed along the waterfront. The evening's only catastrophic injury was the fatal heart attack experienced by a taxi driver caught in the Christopher Street blockade.

The next three nights—Sunday, Monday, and Tuesday—proved increasingly quiet in the Stonewall neighborhood. Gay advocates returned, as did police officers, but the TPF took a less confrontational approach (appearing without riot gear, for example), and any scuffles and violence were isolated events, not the extended riots from the weekend.

Wednesday, July 2, was another matter, however. That night the *Village Voice* released its newest issue for sale, which featured the Smith-Truscott accounts of the weekend riots. While the

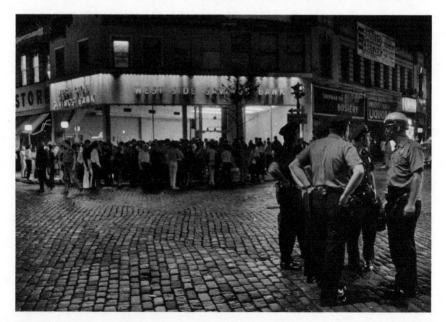

Tactical Police Force officers return to the West Village, July 2, 1969. Violence outside the offices of the Village Voice triggered yet another night of unrest near the Stonewall Inn.

facts of their reporting prompted no major criticism, the tone of the pieces, especially Truscott's, literally provoked another riot. Overall, news coverage of the riots had been slim. Who, news editors asked in 1969, would want to read about homosexuals? No one, most of them decided. *The New York Times* devoted far more ink to the destruction of that wooded gay cruising area in Queens than it did to the gay riots in Greenwich Village, and the *New York Post* had run a playful, punning headline, "No Place for Gaiety," above its brief account of the weekend riots.

In contrast, the *Village Voice* offered extensive coverage, but with homophobic and condescending jargon. Truscott, especially, had laced his article with insensitive humor. "'Gay power' erected its brazen head and spat out a fairy tale," began his story. He continued with a string of demeaning phrases such as "The forces of faggotry," "Wrists were limp, hair was primped," "dyke," "Limp wrists were forgotten," "gay cheerleaders," "If Friday night had been pick-up night, Saturday was date night," "gay tomfoolery," "Sunday fag follies," and "That put a damper on posing and primping."

Belittled. Mocked. Disrespected. And by their own neighborhood's newspaper. Some people advocated burning down the offices of the *Voice*, which stood across Seventh Avenue South from Christopher Park. Instead, recent cycles of protest and police pushback repeated themselves yet again. More broken heads. More injured cops. More trash basket fires. More shattered glass. Another visit by the TPF. This wave of fury was short-lived, lasting not even an hour in length, and by midnight an uneasy peace had settled over the streets of the West Village.

An uneasy peace and an unanswered question: How long would the quiet last?

CHAPTER 8
GAY PRIDE

"To those who wrote to blast me for my refusal to put down the homosexual: The most burdensome problem the homosexual must bear is the stigma placed upon him by an unenlightened and intolerant society."

—ABIGAIL VAN BUREN, advising "compassion and understanding" in her "Dear Abby" column, February 9, 1971

BY THE FOLLOWING MORNING, JULY 3, 1969, CRAIG RODWELL'S mind was on the next protest—the one that would take place the subsequent day in Philadelphia. He had recruited several dozen people to accompany him on a chartered bus to the Annual Reminder, and, on the fourth, passengers buzzed about the Christopher Street happenings during their day trip to Independence Hall. Rodwell and others quickly realized that their annual protest seemed stale and stifled in comparison to the recent Stonewall riots. Some participants ignored protocol and began holding hands as they marched, frustrating protest organizer Frank Kameny. Rodwell further broke with form and defied Kameny's self-designation as the group's only spokesperson.

A poster commemorating the tenth anniversary of the Stonewall riots, 1979. It proclaimed: "Ten Years After Stonewall, Keeping the Spirit Alive."

"Did you hear about what's going on in New York?" he challenged news reporters on the scene. Kameny fumed, but Rodwell recognized, as he rode home, that the Annual Reminders were over. Once again, as he had done during 1965 in Washington, D.C., Rodwell envisioned what should come next. His dream of a gay holiday now had the right occasion to commemorate. Forget the Fourth of July. The gay community had its own declaration of independence to celebrate: the one it had just made on Christopher Street in New York City. In an instant the idea was born for an annual commemorative march in honor of the Stonewall riots.

Rodwell envisioned the first parade taking place on the one-year anniversary of the beginning of the unrest. In fact, he only had to wait a month for the Stonewall uprising to be marked. After the *Village Voice* backlash on July 2, an illusion of calm had settled again over the Christopher Street area. But on July 27, 1969, five hundred or more protesters rallied in Washington Square Park to celebrate the previous month's unrest with speeches about gay rights. Then the crowd marched down nearby Christopher Street to hear parting remarks outside the Stonewall Inn. No violence took place as, for the first time ever, gay men, lesbians, and their supporters marched on New York City streets in public affirmation of gay rights.

A flurry of other activism filled the month between the riots and this first parade. For years a gay rights movement had simmered, thanks to a few dozen activists. Suddenly hundreds of participants materialized. Leaders and doers seemed to be everywhere. Martha Shelley. Marty Robinson. Morty Manford. Vito Russo. Jim O'Brien. Arthur Evans. Arthur Bell. These new advocates for gay rights joined the workhorses of earlier activism, including Frank Kameny, Craig Rodwell, Barbara Gittings, Kay Tobin, and Randy Wicker. Countless other veterans and newcomers took up the cause, too.

New faces brought new ideas, and new groups came

(and went) as part of the creative process. Mattachine Action Committee. Pink Panthers. Gay Liberation Front. The Lavender Menace. Gay Activists Alliance. Lesbian Liberation Front. Some efforts blended gays and lesbians in shared work, but gender tensions led to many efforts more focused on one orientation or the other. Either way, after decades of collective repression, after so many individuals had faced the likelihood of silent, isolated life journeys, gays were eager to gather and celebrate the creation of a supportive community.

Activists rallied, mounted petition drives, founded magazines, printed leaflets, and held meetings. Supporters turned out for dances and fundraisers, for pickets and sit-ins, anything that reinforced the cause. Participants invented a new form of protest—the zap, which was a guerilla-style blend of protest and theater. (One zap targeted a TV appearance by the New York City mayor. Gay rights activists quietly acquired many of the tickets to the taped broadcast and were able to pepper the mayor with questions about gay rights. They also coordinated crowd responses to his evasive

A group photo of the Gay Activists Alliance (GAA) softball team, circa 1970. The GAA used the Greek alphabet letter lambda for its logo to symbolize "the fight for the liberation of all gay people."

answers, forcing the mayor to face a topic he preferred to ignore.) Advocacy groups multiplied and spread to college campuses and big cities and distant communities until there were literally thousands of outposts of the gay rights movement across the country.

On Sunday, June 28, 1970, Rodwell and his team of organizers waited to see if members of the gay community would turn out for the first Christopher Street Liberation Day march. They'd planned for the parade to serve as the finale for the city's first "Gay Pride Week." Earlier events had gone well, but it was one thing to attend the celebration's dances and fundraisers, or even to march along the gay-friendly streets of the West Village as activists had done the previous July. It was quite another to hike more than three miles from Christopher Street through the heart of Manhattan to attend a so-called Gay-In at Central Park, as Rodwell's team planned to do. This was a riskier proposition, and no one knew what to expect. Ridicule? Disdain? Violence? Who would be willing to take a leap of faith to walk that route? Each gay, lesbian, bisexual, and transgender participant would be proclaiming: I am out. Each ally would echo the chorus: We support gay rights.

Rodwell and his coworkers had spent months planning their event, trying to anticipate every potential obstacle. Maps showed where marchers could find bathrooms and pay phones. Marshals learned how to encourage participants to remain nonviolent. Leaflets offered advice on safety. New York's police force was on tap to provide security for the preapproved march, an ironic turn of events for a protest that commemorated the near anarchy the same force had helped to trigger the previous year.

When it came time to start walking, some several hundred people set out. But, by design, the march attracted additional participants from the sidelines as gay onlookers drew courage from the passing parade and became gay demonstrators themselves. Marchers sang. Marchers carried banners that proclaimed their allegiance to the many newly formed gay rights advocacy groups.

Activists participate in the first Christopher Street Liberation Day parade, June 28, 1970.

Marchers hoisted handmade signs with greetings as potentially transformative as HI, MOM!, as affirming as I AM A LESBIAN AND I AM BEAUTIFUL, and as challenging as EVERYTHING YOU THINK WE ARE, WE ARE! And marchers chanted. "Out of the closets and into the streets!" "Two, four, six, eight! Gay is just as good as straight!" "Three, five, seven, nine! Lesbians are mighty fine!" Everywhere there were shouts of "Gay power!"

The energy was infectious. Marchers had set off at a brisk pace, mostly as a form of self-protection, but, to everyone's amazement, no one attacked the throng. "The faces of the crowd show no hostility," observed Leo Skir, a noted poet and one of the parade's crowd-control marshals. Instead he saw "usually blankness, sometimes encouragement." How could supporters on the sidelines resist joining in?

"As we rolled up Sixth Avenue," Rodwell later recalled, the march "just ballooned and ballooned and got more and more thrilling. Half the people were in tears." Those at the rear of the parade could not see its head, for eventually the procession stretched for fifteen city blocks. Those at the front of the march, after reaching their destination in Central Park, looked back and could not see the parade's end. Thousands of people had joined their demonstration. After years of modest success, organizers such as Rodwell, Kameny, and others suddenly found themselves among an army of supporters.

Doric Wilson, a participant in the previous year's riots, had been among the day's original corps of marchers. He later told the film crew for the *Stonewall Uprising* American Experience documentary that he had traveled to the event's starting place hoping, "Please let there be more than ten of us, just please let there be more than ten of us. Because it's all right in the Village, but the minute we cross Fourteenth Street, if there's only ten of us, God knows what's going to happen to us." Now he was finishing the march in the company of thousands. "That's when I knew it had happened," Wilson remembered. "I cannot tell this without tearing up," he admitted. "That's when we knew, we were ourselves for the first time. America thought we were these homosexual monsters and we were so innocent, and oddly enough, we were so American."

Another marcher echoed Wilson's theme: "This was the moment when the closet door was actually opening and the gay community was coming out into the light." Rodwell's dream of celebrating a gay holiday had worked, and not just in New York City. His team had reasoned that if they were going to create a gay holiday, they should make it a national one. Organizers contacted friends in Boston, Chicago, Los Angeles, and San Francisco, and each of those cities hosted gay pride celebrations during 1970, too.

Over the years Rodwell and others nurtured the New York event from seedling to institution. By the tenth anniversary of the riots, in 1979, the parade had doubled in length, filling nearly thirty city blocks as fifty thousand or more participants marched toward Central Park. By the end of the twentieth century, hundreds of thousands took part in the event. The commemorative parades continued to spread from New York to points around the globe, including, by the fifteenth anniversary of the riots, in 1984, twenty-five cities across the United States.

"You can cure yourself, in a day, a minute, a second, with three words, with six. I'm-not-sick—three words. Three words more: I-love-myself."

—LEO SKIR, poet and activist, sharing his advice
to a closeted friend in 1970

To Rodwell's satisfaction—and perhaps partly due to his post-riot leaflet—the Stonewall bar itself collapsed from lack of business only a few months after Seymour Pine's ill-fated raid. Periodically other establishments have capitalized on the fame of the spot and opened bars using the Stonewall name at the historic location. Although the bar's name has lived on, it is the riots sparked outside of it, not the business itself, that has earned annual commemoration.

In the years following 1969, gay rights organizations rose and fell and regrouped to rise again. Their collective efforts inevitably contributed to the movement's forward momentum. Soon gays began advocating for political power, and a few openly gay candidates—such as Harvey Milk in San Francisco in 1977—succeeded in gaining elected office.

For the gay community, the 1970s served as a decade of self-liberation as much as one of political or cultural change. The idea of coming out of the closet took hold. The medical community—under pressure from gay activists—withdrew its pronouncement that homosexuality was a mental illness. Being gay became something to celebrate, to share, to enjoy. Gay bars sprang up that weren't run by the Mafia. Gay bathhouses flourished. Gay attire ran the gamut from straight to hippie to biker-black leather. Surgery offered transformation for transgender individuals. During an era of widespread promiscuity regardless of sexual orientation, many members of the gay community joined the national experiment.

As the era's activists began to make headway on liberalizing local and state laws, they encountered a new obstacle to their work. Or, actually, they encountered a very old one. One institution—the Christian church—had inspired the nation's moral code hundreds of years earlier, a code that later became infused in the nation's legal system. Now that some elements of society—gay and straight—sought to update laws that seemed out of step with modern times, representatives of the conservative Christian faith rushed to defend the rules their beliefs had helped to create.

By the mid-1970s, the gay community, although its individuals

Gay activist and politician Harvey Milk, riding in San Francisco's gay pride parade, June 25, 1978. Five months later, Milk was murdered in a hate crime.

were more liberated, found itself fighting collectively on multiple fronts. Against religious conservatives. Against governing bodies that still discriminated based on sexual orientation. Against ignorance within the straight community. Against the fears that still kept many individuals in the closet. Against the inertia of movement fatigue. Against the unexpected. In 1978, for example, too soon after Harvey Milk's election and service in San Francisco had begun to inspire gays to fight for their rights, his voice was silenced by assassination. Craig Rodwell, of course, knew Milk from their days as lovers in New York City during the previous decade. Milk had been so closeted then that his anxiety over Rodwell's activism had soured their relationship and pushed Rodwell to attempt suicide. Now Milk's own activism had cost him his life.

Come out of the closet, the politicized Milk had urged. "Come out, come out, come out," his friends recalled him imploring in his speeches. "You have to come out." Taped messages found after his murder echoed that theme: "If a bullet should enter my brain," Milk had suggested in an eerie premonition of his death, "let that bullet destroy every closet door." His calls for openness echoed in the void left by his passing.

California activists struggled to find meaning in work that had lost its most gifted spokesperson. Organizers there and elsewhere tried to keep pushing against conservative forces to end discrimination. Rodwell and others continued to organize parades and urge gay pride. But for many gays in the 1970s, being out of the closet served as reward enough, and individuals reveled in their ability to find partners, have casual sex, experiment. For them, enjoying these newfound personal freedoms took the place of fighting for further collective ones. And why not? Gays could finally begin to be themselves, uninhibited. Why not just live it up for a change? Just live it up.

And then came AIDS.

CHAPTER 9

GAY PLAGUE

> "*Everyone detected with AIDS should be tattooed in the upper forearm, to protect common-needle users, and on the buttocks, to prevent the victimization of other homosexuals.*"
> —WILLIAM F. BUCKLEY, JR.,
> conservative commentator,
> in a 1986 opinion piece for *The New York Times*

AND THEN CAME AIDS.

Acquired immunodeficiency syndrome. A disease that took more than a year to name and even longer to understand. A disease that had been quietly infiltrating the gay community during the previous decade—especially in such urban centers as New York City and San Francisco—until thousands of gay men had been infected by it before the first symptoms of illness began to gain attention in the spring of 1981. Tens of thousands more would be stricken during the period of uncertainty and neglect that followed a dawning awareness: something strange and even sinister was making members of the gay community seriously ill.

Activists and mourners gather on the National Mall in Washington, D.C., April 25, 1993. Panels from the AIDS Quilt (spread out below) commemorated victims of what some called a gay plague because so many of its first victims were gay men.

A man offers a solemn drum beat to accompany a candlelight march for victims of AIDS, May 2, 1983.

The symptoms were so bizarre—purple, cancer-linked spots on seemingly healthy young men; inexplicable cases of pneumonia; night sweats; debilitating throat infections—and all the suggested treatments were so ineffective that no one seemed sure what to do. And then the people began to die. All of them. Death claimed anyone who exhibited signs of the illness, often within a matter of months.

When gay men became sick with AIDS, the harshest conservatives dismissed their plight as God's will, a just punishment for unnatural behavior. "The poor homosexuals," intoned Patrick J. Buchanan in 1983. This conservative political commentator and former Republican presidential staffer observed: "They have declared war upon nature, and now nature is exacting an awful retribution." PRAISE GOD FOR AIDS, read cards distributed several years later in Georgia by J. B. Stoner, an infamous segregationist.

Ronald Reagan, a Republican who had been elected president with the help of conservative voters, deferred to the interests of his political base and disregarded warnings of an unusual illness spreading among gay men. Even before the arrival of AIDS, Reagan had begun cutting research and prevention funds from the very agencies that were designed to control and cure mysterious diseases. Money remained tight despite the continuing spread of the disease. Not until 1987, near the end of his second term in office, did the president even mention AIDS in a public address. By the end of that year just over 50,000 Americans—mostly gay men—had been diagnosed with the illness, and barely 2,000 of them were still alive. Another 30,000 cases would be reported by the end of the next year and hundreds of thousands more after that.

Once again the old enemy of silence became a force in the life of the gay community. Originally it had haunted gay men and lesbians as they concealed their sexual orientation, confined to virtual closets and surrounded by the lies they had to tell and live in order to conceal their secret. Then it was the silence of heterosexuals who refused to acknowledge the validity of demands for gay community members to be treated as equals. Now the silence came from the government as it failed to acknowledge the urgency of the health crisis preying upon gay men.

Further complications arose among gay men themselves. Many gays were still exploring newfound opportunities for self-expression and they chafed against calls from within (and beyond) for them to abandon newly acquired freedoms. Stop having sex? End promiscuity? Always use condoms? Close the bathhouses? What kind of homophobic conspiracy was this? And so, out of ignorance, out of denial, out of sheer force of habit, infections continued to spread and fatalities mounted.

The illness drained the rolls of Broadway. AIDS removed creative and successful voices from the worlds of fashion, commerce, art, dance, and literature. It depleted the ranks of activists, taking the lives of Marty Robinson, Vito Russo, Morty Manford, and countless other leaders in the movement. Craig Rodwell escaped being infected with AIDS, but he, too, died young, succumbing to stomach cancer at age fifty-two, just a few days before New York's 1993 gay pride march.

Having long since relinquished his role as event organizer,

Rodwell had lived to see twenty-two commemorative parades. Although the enduring parades may have comforted him, he surely must have grieved over the toll AIDS took on the people around him and on his life's work of advocacy. During an era when the most extreme voices suggested branding the infected and corralling them into quarantine, it seemed as if all the momentum from the 1960s, from the Stonewall riots, from the post-Stonewall awakening, all of that momentum was at risk.

Even the perennial New York City gay rights parade signaled a retreat by reversing course in 1983 so that participants marched toward the relative safety of Washington Square Park in Greenwich Village and away from the citywide gathering spot of Central Park. As the years wore on, the parade once envisioned as an expression of gay pride took on an almost funereal function. A commemoration for ghosts of faces suddenly absent; a march undertaken by survivors, many of whom felt their own lives at risk.

By the mid-1980s—some three years into the AIDS crisis—the threat and horror of the illness began to inspire not just grief but fresh waves of activism. In 1985, Cleve Jones, one of Harvey Milk's closest friends and supporters in San Francisco, imagined the commemorative project that came to be known as the AIDS Quilt. The quilt, which first went on display in 1987, has grown to hold about fifty thousand panels that honor individuals who have died from AIDS.

The same year the quilt debuted, members of the gay community and straight supporters on the East Coast established the AIDS Coalition to Unleash Power, or ACT UP. Among its key founders was the influential playwright Larry Kramer, an insistent early voice for community action over AIDS. The tragedy of AIDS helped to erase old tensions between lesbians and gay men, and lesbians joined this and other efforts to help the illness's mostly gay male victims.

ACT UP blended all the dimensions of past gay activism—zaps and theater and creativity and wit and anger—into a potent force for change. "Silence = Death" became the group's trademark slogan, accompanied by a pink triangle that echoed the badge the Nazis had forced homosexuals to wear. Silence equals death. Protesters directed ambitious, forceful acts of civil disobedience against institutions seen as inattentive to the AIDS crisis, including the Federal Drug Administration, the New York Stock Exchange, the pharmaceutical industry, the Catholic Church, the National Institutes of Health, the American Medical Association, the White House, and more.

The Reagan administration's lack of attention to AIDS research, funding, and patient care continued during the presidency of George H. W. Bush, so ACT UP persisted with its protests. On October 11, 1992, for example, during its so-called Ashes Action, thousands of chanting protesters marched to the perimeter fence around the White House so that they could toss the ashes of loved ones who had died from AIDS onto the White House lawn. "History will recall, Reagan and Bush did nothing at all," they chanted. Despite such an aggressive display of grief, AIDS infections and deaths escalated. The disease no longer affected only the gay

An ACT UP advertisement, 1989.

community. AIDS also spread through illegal drug use and blood transfusions, having an impact on the whole world's population.

"We die. They do nothing!
We die. They do nothing!"

—A signature chant from
ACT UP demonstrations

Political disinterest in AIDS finally ended in the spring of 1992 when presidential hopeful Bill Clinton embraced the concerns of the gay community. "I have a vision, and you're a part of it," the Democrat told the citizens who were just beginning to identify themselves with the acronym LGBT, which stood for lesbian, gay, bisexual, and transgender. (Some advocates have since added a Q at the end of the acronym, representing the catchall words *queer* and *questioning.*) "I believe we're all a part of the same community," Clinton added, "and we'd better start behaving as if we are." In November 1992, one month after ACT UP participants had tossed the ashes of AIDS victims over the White House fence, Clinton defeated his Republican incumbent opponent. The new president owed his victory, in part, to the active political support of the LGBT community.

When Clinton took office, members of that community still faced a host of legal and cultural barriers. Sodomy laws banned same-sex acts, even in the privacy of one's bedroom, in more than half of the country's states plus the nation's capital. Military service members earned automatic dishonorable discharges if their same-sex preferences became known. Few churches openly embraced gay and lesbian members, and almost none endorsed the idea of ordaining them to lead congregations. Members of the gay community received no additional protection from acts of violence motivated by homophobia.

Worst of all, thousands of gay men continued to die from a disease that had assumed the proportions of a plague. Annual reported deaths from AIDS in the United States had climbed from their beginning of 618 in 1982 to nearly 7,000 in 1985 and more than 30,000 per year by the end of 1990. In 1992, ten years after the naming of AIDS, a quarter million Americans were infected with the condition, and an ever-growing number were dying from it each year. Nearly 40,000 died during the 1992 presidential election year alone.

This seemingly unstoppable escalation of AIDS infections and deaths—which served to increase the terror associated with the disease—came to an end during the Clinton presidency. Clinton brought no conservative social prejudices or political constraints to his science agenda, and he unleashed hundreds of millions of dollars of federal money to study and treat the disease. Within three years, scientists had identified a potent drug cocktail that essentially halted the progression of AIDS. It wasn't a cure, but it was a life-saving Band-Aid. Annual deaths from AIDS in the United States peaked in 1995 with 48,979 fatalities, then began to decline precipitously. The rate of infection dropped, too, thanks to an accompanying burst of funding for AIDS awareness and prevention. For all intents and purposes, the contraction of AIDS stopped being an automatic death sentence, and the illness lost much of its political toxicity, although it remains a serious public health concern.

During this same period the U.S. Supreme Court began considering gay rights. In 1986, seven years before Clinton became president, the court had shocked the gay community with its

Bowers v. Hardwick decision. The 5-4 ruling upheld laws in twenty-four states plus the nation's capital that banned sodomy, or nonvaginal sexual intercourse, even between consenting adults in their own dwellings. The ruling didn't require states to ban sodomy, though, and within three years seventeen of them had decriminalized the practice.

In 2003, two years after Clinton left the White House, the Supreme Court dramatically reversed itself. In *Lawrence v. Texas*, by a vote of 6 to 3, the majority opinion declared a Texas sodomy law unconstitutional. It rejected earlier legal arguments and expressly endorsed the rights of gender-matched couples to experience the same freedoms of sexual expression that heterosexuals enjoyed. Because the ruling came from the highest court in the land, it not only applied to the law in Texas but made every other sodomy law in individual states unconstitutional. At that moment, homosexuality ceased to be a crime for private citizens in the United States of America.

Members of the armed forces received no protection from the Supreme Court ruling, however, and gay servicemen and women remained subject to dismissal if their sexual orientations became known. The practice of stripping dishonorably discharged veterans of all benefits meant that soldiers such as Vietnam War combatant Leonard Matlovich would, among other consequences, be denied the honor of burial in Arlington National Cemetery. Matlovich summed up his experience as a service member in one sentence: "When I was in the military they gave me a medal for killing two men and a discharge for loving one." These words became the epitaph on his tombstone after he died in 1988 from AIDS.

Candidate Clinton had pledged to stop discrimination against gays and lesbians who served in the armed forces, and, soon after becoming president, he issued an executive order intended to protect them. He called his policy "Don't Ask, Don't Tell," meaning, we won't ask if you are gay, and you won't tell us if you are. In other words, gays could serve in the military, but only if they remained closeted. This policy of uneasy half measures lasted eighteen years, with conservative military and political leaders refusing to condone the presence of openly gay service members in the U.S. military. Not until the end of 2010, two years after the election of the next Democratic president, Barack Obama, was the policy struck down while Democrats controlled both chambers of Congress. The following year the military phased out its restrictions, and gay men and women earned the right to serve their country without constraint.

Finally, it seemed, the decades of death and denial and darkness were beginning to lift.

CHAPTER 10

THE
RAINBOW

> "We, the people, declare today that the most evident
> of truths—that all of us are created equal—is the
> star that guides us still; just as it guided our forebears
> through Seneca Falls, and Selma, and Stonewall."
>
> —BARACK OBAMA, second inaugural address,
> January 21, 2013

IN 1978, SAN FRANCISCO POLITICIAN HARVEY MILK HAD
phoned one of his friends and said, "Gilbert, we need a logo."
Gay rights had become a hot topic in California, and a unifying
emblem seemed in order. When Gilbert Baker's rainbow-striped
banner was unfurled soon after, Milk reportedly told him, "This
will be the most important thing that you ever do in your life."
"And it was," says Baker, who has watched six horizontal stripes
of color—red, orange, yellow, green, blue, and purple—become
as iconic a symbol of gay pride as the parades initiated by Craig
Rodwell. For decades now, literally marching under that banner,
activists have fought on behalf of AIDS victims, argued for the
end of "Don't Ask, Don't Tell," and, particularly in recent years,
campaigned for marriage equality.

*Marchers carry a mile-long rainbow-striped banner to commemorate the
twenty-fifth anniversary of the Stonewall riots during the gay pride parade,
New York City, June 26, 1994.*

When the fight for same-sex marriage started, religious conservatives and other opponents of the idea wielded considerable power in federal and state governments. Furthermore, most Americans agreed with their view: marriage was a sacred right reserved for heterosexuals only. Gay activists won their first victory in 1993 when the state court of Hawaii ruled that gays could legally marry there thanks to a clause in the state constitution that prohibited discrimination on the basis of gender. Conservative members of Congress, fearing that other states might legalize gay marriage, too, passed the Defense of Marriage Act in 1996. Eager to avoid a reelection fight that year over gay rights, President Bill Clinton signed the legislation into law. The act set forth an official definition of marriage as a bond that could only be established between a man and a woman.

Undeterred, a handful of advocates for marriage equality kept pressing forward with their arguments in favor of same-sex unions. Much of their work took place in the courts. Same-sex couples were denied basic civil rights, they argued, because they lacked the legal benefits that come with marriage, everything from lower tax rates to the right to visit a dying spouse in a hospital. These champions of gay marriage hoped to challenge the constitutionality of the Defense of Marriage Act by pursuing a legal strategy that would take the matter to the United States Supreme Court. This plan took patience and endless effort, but it began to work.

By 2012, for the first time ever, a majority of Americans polled nationally supported gay marriage. Soon after, Barack Obama became the first president in United States history to voice his support for the rights of all citizens to marry, regardless of sexual orientation. Following his reelection later that year, he emphasized his commitment to marriage equality in his second inaugural address: "For if we are truly created equal, then surely the love we commit to one another must be equal as well."

A few months later, on June 26, 2013, the nation's highest court issued its 5–4 *United States v. Windsor* decision that struck down key provisions of the Defense of Marriage Act. The federal government could no longer deny the rights of marriage to same-sex couples. Furthermore, states probably couldn't either. Almost immediately states and their courts began to question, repeal, overturn, and end their bans on gay marriage. In the fall of 2014, the Supreme Court chose not to reconsider a series of lower court rulings that supported marriage equality, thus allowing those rulings to stand in all affected states. Within weeks, people in thirty-six states could marry partners of the same gender. Then on June 26, 2015, the Supreme Court announced a landmark 5–4 decision that established same-sex marriage as a national right.

Advocates at a kiss-in to promote gay rights gather outside of the Church of Jesus Christ of Latter Day Saints in San Diego, California, July 22, 2009.

In 1966, three years before the Stonewall riots, a Miami television station produced a program called *The Homosexual*. The broadcast included an interview with Richard Enman, president of the Florida chapter of the Mattachine Society. "There has been much to-do," said Enman, when asked about the legal rights sought by homosexuals, "that the Society was in favor of the legalization of marriage between homosexuals, and the adoption of children, and such as that, and that is not at all factual at all. Homosexuals do not want that," Enman asserted. He added: "You might find some fringe character someplace who says that that's what he wants." At the time Enman and his organization sought something more fundamental—the same thing rioters sought three years later outside a gay bar in Greenwich Village: the right to personal respect.

That quest for social justice had been kindled in the 1950s, nurtured during the 1960s, transformed by the Stonewall riots, and matured into a movement that continued through the twentieth century and was carried forward into the new millennium. Now the history of American gay rights unfolds through the current events of the nation. Today members of the LGBT community expect to enjoy the same equal rights that other segments of the American family have fought for—and may still be fighting to achieve—whether as early revolutionaries, women, immigrants, African Americans, or Native Americans.

Did the Stonewall riots spark the gay rights movement? It's a frequently repeated claim, but one that discounts the wider scope of history. A campaign for gay rights had existed for decades by the time of the riots. Gay rights didn't start with Stonewall. The groundwork undertaken by those pre-Stonewall pioneers made it possible for a larger, more radical movement to flourish after the riots. Without a doubt the riots served as a catalyst, as a galvanizing experience for future activists, a number of whom participated in them or were immediately influenced by their occurrence.

As important as the riots were themselves, the annual tribute Craig Rodwell conceived to commemorate them has become an even more transformative force. Those perennial marches captured the spirit of the liberation movement that ignited during a routine police raid in New York City. Christopher Street Liberation Day was the name Rodwell gave to his gay holiday parade, and that was what he commemorated. Not a corrupt gay bar, but the spirit of freedom that seized a people who found themselves united on a hot, moonlit night. These annual parades, timed to fall on or near the last Sunday in June, outlasted every other initiative that followed the Stonewall riots.

In the decades since, the parade in New York City has honored its origins, commemorated losses, and marked the changes of the eras. In 1996, gay uniformed members of the city's police force joined the march down Fifth Avenue for the first time. In later years, so did legally married same-sex couples, openly gay members of the military, and openly gay members of the clergy. In 2014, this parade for the first time included a contingent of uniformed members of the Boy Scouts of America, commemorating their organization's decision the previous year to allow gays to participate openly as scouts.

"We'll be gay until everyone has forgotten that it's an issue. Then we'll begin to be complete."

—CARL WITTMAN, from his "Gay Manifesto,"
authored shortly before the Stonewall Riots

Fights for social justice—whether for fair employment, marriage equality, or tolerance—remain just as challenging as past quests for reform. Forward momentum is inevitably tempered by pushback from forces that disapprove of change. For every troop with members who supported the inclusion of gay Boy Scouts, for example, there were others that opposed them, some so vehemently that they withdrew their chapters from the national group entirely.

Young gays continue to live in a world where staying closeted may seem like the safest option, where the promise of the "It

Gets Better" campaign may seem like a distant possibility offered by people who've already grown up and crossed into safer territory, where teasing and bullying can be just as hurtful and just as frightening as they were to members of the Stonewall generation. In 2009, Congress passed the Matthew Shepard & James Byrd, Jr., Hate Crimes Prevention Act, which makes it a federal crime to commit violence fueled by the dislike of someone's gender or sexual orientation, but it can't eliminate bias.

And yet the world around today's American youths is noticeably more tolerant than it was for their counterparts in the 1960s. Out-of-the-closet role models star in movies, appear as key characters in television programs, sing hit songs, play professional sports, run for political office, portray roles in video games, and fill the pages of literature for children of all ages. Countless young people are members of families with same-sex parents. Others are enjoying the freedom to explore their gender identities during adolescence in ways that would have seemed almost unimaginable to the cross-dressing warriors who helped to storm the Stonewall in 1969.

Change does come.

Seymour Pine, the police inspector who inadvertently set off the riots, lived until 2010, reaching the age of ninety-one. In his later years he apologized for leading his ill-fated June raid. Speaking about the young people caught up in the police raids of the 1960s, Pine once remarked, "They were kids. You knew you could ruin them for life. And you felt bad that you were part of this, when you knew they broke the law, but what kind of law was that?" Realizing the role that the Stonewall riots played in gay history he would later comment, "If what I did helped gay people, then I'm glad."

The character of the riots themselves—that empowered, no-holds-barred, creative approach to protest—lived on during the years of struggle that followed. That late-night call for equal justice inspired the zaps of the 1970s. It fueled the channeled rage of ACT UP. It converted a lengthening list of names into a memorial quilt so large that it could carpet the Washington Mall and crack open the heart of a nation. The spirit that emerged outside a Mafia-run bar in 1969 became the pulse of the gay community and inspired not just an annual parade but ways to express gay pride in individual lives.

"Stonewall happens every day," longtime activist Virginia Apuzzo has observed. "When you go to a Pride march and you see people standing on the side of the road watching and then someone takes that first step off the curb to join the marchers, that's Stonewall all over again."

In 1991, Barbara Gittings, one of the earliest pre-Stonewall pioneers for gay rights, noted that the "stigma attached to being gay" continued to serve as "the major reason we're still in business" as activists. She added, "I hope we're going to go out of business as a social change movement before I end my lifetime." Gittings herself devoted decades of her life to the promotion of literature for young people by and about gays, correcting a deficit in library collections that she had encountered during her own childhood. Although she died in 2007, six years before the U.S. Supreme Court pulled the foundations out from under the Defense of Marriage Act, Gittings lived to enjoy a world that she and fellow activists could only dream of decades earlier, one of far more acceptance, far more opportunity, far less stigma.

"I have just marched through a little tunnel of history on the little scenic railway that is my life," wrote the poet Leo Skir after attending the inaugural Gay Pride parade of 1970. "Things will never be the same. Gay kids will have kissing contests, restaurants, resorts, organizations. We are following the blacks," he observed. "And we will follow, entering, perhaps, the same time as women." Looking ahead, he predicted, "A Woman's History of the World, A Gay History of the World. Something like that will come out."

And so it has, with increasing frequency. Scholars study gay history. Books rush to keep pace with changing gay rights. Journalists report almost daily another state where same-sex couples can marry, another group or sport or opportunity that now encompasses participation regardless of gender orientation, a fresh instance where tolerance and inclusion of gays becomes a matter of respect and expectation, not a distant dream.

Yes, there are setbacks, but, with each advance, that LGBT rainbow symbol of diversity becomes ever more an overarching canopy that can embrace the entire American family. Gay and straight. Black and white. Immigrant and native born. Male and female. Transgender and anything else. Ever growing, always stretching. Forever pushing toward that goal of creating a more perfect union.

One nation, indivisible, with liberty and justice for all.

A "For Rent" sign sits in the window of the former Stonewall Inn, September 1969. The Mafia-run gay bar went out of business within months of the Stonewall riots.

Sylvia Rivera and Marsha Johnson (holding umbrella) advoca
end sexual orientation discrimination in New York City, 19
Like many veterans of the Stonewall riots, Rivera and John
became activists for gay rights. They were pioneers in the
for the freedom to live unbounded by the gender of their bi
a right still being sought in the twenty-first century

AN EPILOGUE

The door still beckons.

It swings open, and people walk back in time, remembering when bodies pulsed to the beat of the final year in a tumultuous decade.

Living on the edge of revolution.

And then they made history.

The door swings open, and people walk into the future. A future filled with tumultuous times.

A future where anything can happen.

A future where people make history.

Marriage equality. Done. Won. Declared the law of the land by the Supreme Court. June 26, 2015.

Celebrate the day.

The pulse goes on. The dreams go on.

The work goes on.

Job security regardless of sexual orientation or gender identity.

Parental rights for same-sex couples.

The right to live where everyone else lives.

Transgender rights. Transgender love. Transgender acceptance.

Wait for it.

Watch for it.

Work for it.

The door still beckons.

People walk through that door to celebrate change.

People walk through that door to make change.

Pay attention.

Keep walking.

Go make history.

A NOTE FROM THE AUTHOR

The woman leaned in, over a table filled with my books, and whispered, "Could you please write something like this for young people about the history of gay rights?"

It was 2010, and I was signing books at a festival in South Dakota when a stranger uttered this plea, or words to that effect. Earnest. Expectant. Her entreaty rising from the depths of some untold story. My heart yearned to say yes. In my head I imagined one moment in time: *Stonewall*. But my response was noncommittal. I'd wanted to write about the Stonewall riots for years, but was I the right person to explore this history? I saw myself as a straight outsider, an interloper when it came to the topic of gay rights. And even if I did write such a book, would anyone, as things stood in 2010, dare to publish it?

The next day I learned about the death of Tyler Clementi. A college student slightly younger than my own college-aged sons. Newly arrived on campus. Celebrating his coming out as a gay male. Then so demoralized following his betrayal by his unsympathetic roommate that he felt compelled to jump to his death from the George Washington Bridge. Tyler Clementi died on September 22, 2010. Upon hearing the news, I pushed old hesitations aside and pledged to write about gay rights history. This book is written in memory of Tyler and in honor of all young people whose lives are challenged by homophobia.

I was only eleven years old in 1969 when the Stonewall riots occurred. Too young to hear about Stonewall, too young to even know much about sexuality or same-sex attractions. Ten years later, I found myself living in the city where the riots had happened. When I visited Greenwich Village and walked down Christopher Street, past the former Stonewall Inn, I witnessed the vibrant gay life that thrived along this corridor during those heady days post-Stonewall and pre-AIDS. Public displays of affection. Shop windows stocked with adult-entertainment merchandise for same-sex partners. Cross-dressing. And leather. Lots of leather.

Then, less than a decade later, it was as if the hand of death had draped the Village with invisible black shrouds. AIDS changed everything. A palpable sense of grief and fear and anger hung over Christopher Street. A sense of disorder and stolen victory. And terrible, terrible loss. So many people suffering. So many people gone.

Someone I knew from college was among the young people who had found love and acceptance on Christopher Street. Michael Riesenberg also found death there. Too young to have witnessed Stonewall, Mike did not live to celebrate the culminating torrent of gay rights victories that would follow decades later. Robbed of his health, robbed of his potential, robbed of his longevity, Mike died on June 16, 1993, at the age of thirty-four. I write this book in his memory and as a tribute to all the people who have died because of AIDS.

Half a lifetime since the events of 1969, I write to celebrate the survivors, too. Those who remember Stonewall and those who've barely heard of it. The people who align with every shade of the LGBT gay pride rainbow and the people who are their friends and allies.

I write for the individuals who persevered in the struggle and those who've benefited from it. Those I've never known and those who've become some of my closest friends, including Mike Bess, to whom this book is dedicated. Mike has encouraged me in all my writing, but he took a personal interest in this story. Born in the early 1950s, he came of age with a generation whose lives could have turned out differently. Closeted. Constrained. Conflicted. Making do with halting steps toward half-measures of equality. But history turned out differently.

Because then came Stonewall.

ACKNOWLEDGMENTS

Every book creates its own research journey, and each journey accumulates its own debt of gratitude. *Stonewall* started thanks to the support of friends, especially Mike Bess, but also Hester White and fellow nonfiction author Sue Macy. All three encouraged me to see myself as the person meant to explore this history. I perfected the earliest versions of my text with advice from Mike Bess, Sue Macy, and the members of my writing critique group—Pam Beres, Georgia Beaverson, Judy Bryan, Elizabeth Fixmer, and Jamie Swenson. I remain grateful to Ken Wright, vice president and publisher of Viking Children's Books, for giving me the chance to turn those early ideas into this book.

The archival work I undertook during two periods of research at the New York Public Library remains memorable not just for how much it contributed to this project but as one of my career-favorite archival experiences. I particularly appreciated the help of reference archivist Tal Nadan; she guided my work on-site and off. On my second visit to the Manuscripts and Archives Division I spent the better part of a week immersing myself in the extensive papers of Craig Rodwell. During this trip, I flagged hundreds of pages of documents for further review and spent many weeks later on culling through copies of them to create a critical part of the research framework for this book.

I gained additional insights during companion work at the National History Archive of the Lesbian, Gay, Bisexual & Transgender Community Center in New York City. Archivist Rich Wandel graciously shared his collections and expertise with me during a pair of visits to this history-filled center. I particularly enjoyed being able to review Wandel's own photos from the post-Stonewall era, and I am delighted to present one of them in this book.

Every research project has a reading list, and David Carter's *Stonewall: The Riots That Sparked the Gay Revolution* proved to be both an early and an essential addition to mine. All researchers of this subject are indebted to Carter for constructing the first comprehensive account of these events, and his work remains the definitive history of the riots. The accompanying bibliography highlights other key sources for my project, but special mention should be made here of two iconic works by Randy Shilts: *The Mayor of Castro Street* plus *And the Band Played On.* The former title documents Harvey Milk's life, work, and death; the latter captures the earliest history of AIDS, a disease that silenced yet another brilliant voice when it claimed Shilts's life.

Pop culture and current events kept me company on my research journey, too. Never before have I clipped so many reference-related news articles about a topic. It seemed as if I could barely keep up with history, and, indeed, the latest steps of the march toward gender-orientation equality, most notably marriage equality, eluded capture in time for publication in this volume. For pop culture, I combed both the past and the present. My recreational soundtrack became the equivalent of a Stonewall 1969 jukebox full of popular tunes, and for months I filled my evenings with films and documentaries that captured the 1960s, gay culture, and social history.

By the time I sat down to write, I felt as if I was living in that earlier era. My writing journey, which Ken Wright made possible through his belief in this project, was completed thanks to the collaborative insight of project editor Catherine Frank. Her wisdom and encouragement helped me turn my aspirations for this book into their best possible expression. Ken and Catherine were ably assisted by the very talented Alex Ulyett. Many thanks to project designer Kate Renner and art director Denise Cronin for turning text into type, complete with an inspired (and inspiring) cover and an interior layout that animates the Stonewall riots despite the history's thin photo resources. I'm grateful to the Penguin Young Readers Group sales and marketing teams for helping this title find its audience. Nothing makes an author happier than for a book to make a difference to a reader. Kudos, all.

Every book comes into being thanks not just to active participants but to those who witness its creation. Personal support proved as critical as ever—from my parents and other family members to my critique partners to friends, including Greg and Elizabeth Hopper, who graciously housed me twice during my New York research.

This time, though, I also wrote in the company of ghosts. It was as if a chorus of witnesses to history peered over my shoulders, fueled my fingers, and stirred my heart. *Write*, they seemed to say. *Keep working. Write about us so that our struggles can be remembered, so that others can draw strength from our labors, so that our lives were not foreshortened in vain.* These voices helped inspire the creative nonfiction prologue for this book and every word that follows.

One of the last facts I checked for this project was the birth year of Michael Riesenberg, that college friend who died from AIDS when he was thirty-four years old. For verification I contacted Fred Burwell, the archivist for our alma mater, Beloit College. Fred's same-day reply contained not just the year of Mike's birth, 1958, but its date, July 29. I could have chosen any day during the previous four years to confirm this detail, but without realizing it I had chosen to think about Mike on the very date when, except for the vagaries of AIDS and fate, he would have celebrated his fifty-sixth birthday.

On July 29, 2014, I read Fred's reply, felt chills march up my arms, marked the rise of goose bumps across my back, sensed the spirits of history fluttering about my shoulders, and wished Mike a happy birthday. Then I cried.

I wrote this book in the company of ghosts.

SOURCE NOTES

Jacket

"We've got to stand up . . .": Carter, *Stonewall*, 218.

Chapter One—Flash Point

"The door of the Stonewall . . .": Carter, *Stonewall*, 69.

"Why they don't just round us all up . . .": Hirshman, *Victory*, 20.

"It was the best place . . .": Levin, "The Gay Anger Behind the Riots."

"There was a generally up mood in the place . . .": "The Night They Raided the Stonewall," *Gay Activist*.

Chapter Two—The Closet

"When you left bars . . .": *Crosby*, "The Stonewall Riot Remembered."

"We couldn't have them tight enough . . .": Rodwell, Oral history interviews, Folder 2, 6.

"Just holding hands . . .": Rodwell, Oral history interviews, Folder 2, 2.

"We are the Village queens . . .": Rodwell, Oral history interviews, Folder 2, 1.

"found Nirvana . . .": *Stonewall Uprising* transcript, 8.

"have-nothing-to-lose types.": *Stonewall Uprising* transcript, 9.

"Here comes Lillian.": Jerry Hoose, *Stonewall Uprising* transcript, 16.

"Mind you socks didn't count . . .": *Stonewall Uprising* transcript, 11.

"Keep moving, faggot . . .": Rodwell, Oral history interviews, Folder 2, 10.

"If You're Gay, Go Away.": Rodwell, Oral history interviews, Folder 4, 97.

"The closet door was so tight . . .": Carter, *Stonewall*, 49.

"I was just so excited . . ." "This was the last one . . ." and "Let's do it . . .": Rodwell, Oral history interviews, Folder 2, 17.

"Homosexuals Are American . . ." "Homosexuals Ask for Equality . . ." and "Stop Cruel and Unusual . . .": Craig Rodwell Papers, Box 14, Photos, paper set #4.

"created quite a stir . . .": *Before Stonewall*.

Chapter Three—Shut It Down

"For me, there was no bar . . .": *Stonewall Uprising* transcript, 1.

"nothing illegal, per se . . .": Carter, *Stonewall*, 195.

"There's a certain hastiness . . .": D'Arcangelo, *The Homosexual Handbook*, 130.

"On Wednesday and Thursday nights . . .": Di Brienza, "Stonewall Incident."

"everything comes together . . .": Carter, *Stonewall*, 259.

Chapter Four—Raid!

"The police weren't letting us dance . . .": *Stonewall Uprising* transcript, 27.

"Police! We're taking the place.": Carter, *Stonewall*, 137.

"The place is under arrest.": *Stonewall Uprising* transcript, 1.

"I headed for the bathroom . . .": Carter, *Stonewall*, 138.

"It'll be over in a short time.": *Stonewall Uprising* transcript, 1.

"Get your ass over to the Stonewall . . .": Carter, *Stonewall*, 139.

"Together we stood vigil. . .": Manford.

"Usually, when we went to work . . .": Carter, *Stonewall*, 147.

"Hello there, fella.": Carter, *Stonewall*, 145.

"there was a feeling in the air . . .": Rodwell, Oral history interviews, Folder 2, 66.

"Things started off small . . .": *Stonewall Uprising* transcript, 21.

"Gay Power!": Carter, *Stonewall*, 147.

"There is a limit, . . .": Di Brienza, "Stonewall Incident."

"Why don't you guys do something?!": Carter, *Stonewall*, 151.

"Dirty copper!" and "Let's pay them off!": Carter, *Stonewall*, 156.

"Word of the raid passed through . . .": Carter, *Stonewall*, 149.

"just drop [the prisoners] at the Sixth . . .": Smith, "Full Moon over the Stonewall."

"We didn't have the manpower . . .": *Stonewall Uprising* transcript, 2.

"You could see the fear . . .": Di Brienza, "Stonewall Incident."

Chapter Five—Revolution

"You could hear screaming . . ." and "It was terrifying . . .": *Stonewall Uprising* transcript, 23.

"Let's go inside . . ." "You want to come in?" and "In goes me.": Smith, "Full Moon over the Stonewall."

"That's when it really started . . .": Rodwell, Oral history interviews, Folder 2, 68.

"Pigs!" and "Faggot cops!": Smith, "Full Moon over the Stonewall."

"Gay power!": Truscott, "Gay Power Comes to Sheridan Square."

"Occupy—take over . . .": "Queen Power," *RAT*.

"Our goal was to hurt those police . . .": *Stonewall Uprising* transcript, 23.

"There was joy . . .": *Stonewall Uprising* transcript, 22.

"Ah, what the hell! . . .": Carter, *Stonewall*, 161.

"The cops inside . . .": "Queen Power," *RAT*.

"The door crashes open . . .": Smith, "Full Moon over the Stonewall."

"We were shocked . . .": *Stonewall Uprising* transcript, 22.

"I'd been waiting . . .": Carter, *Stonewall*, 179.

"The orgy was taking place . . .": "Queen Power," *RAT*.

"It was the queens . . .": Leitsch, "Gay Riots in the Village."

"I was sure we were gonna . . .": Carter, *Stonewall*, 170.

"Aren't you guys scared? . . .": Smith, "Full Moon over the Stonewall."

"The kids were really scared about . . .": "Queen Power," *RAT*.

"You knew that the first shot . . ." and "Staten Island all alone . . .": *Stonewall Uprising*" transcript, 24.

"Nobody fire! . . .": Carter, *Stonewall*, 172.

Chapter Six—Street Wars

"In the civil rights movement . . .": *Stonewall Uprising* transcript, 2.

"When I heard the sirens . . .": Carter, *Stonewall*, 173.

"There were more people . . .": Carter, *Stonewall*, 174.

"Riot pigs.": "Queen Power," *RAT*.

"These guys had helmets . . .": Carter, *Stonewall*, 175.

"We were like a Hydra . . .": *Stonewall Uprising* transcript, 26.

"Years and years . . .": Carter, *Stonewall*, 179.

"Gay power! . . .": Carter, *Stonewall*, 178.

"You didn't want to get hit. . .": Carter, *Stonewall*, 171.

"We are the Village Girls . . .": *Stonewall Uprising* transcript, 26.

"They got me in the back . . .": Carter, *Stonewall*, 177.

"totally humiliated . . .": Carter, *Stonewall*, 175.

"took bats and just busted . . .": *Stonewall Uprising* transcript, 26.

Chapter Seven—The Awakening

"I thought, my God, we're going to . . .": Hirshman, *Victory*, 101.

"Oh my God, I am not alone . . .": *Stonewall Uprising* transcript, 1.

"We became a people . . .": *Stonewall Uprising* transcript, 30.

"People are beginning to realize . . .": Levin, "The Gay Anger Behind the Riots."

"We knew that this was a moment . . .": *Stonewall Uprising* transcript, 27.

"will go down in history as the first time . . .": Rodwell, "Get the Mafia and the Cops out of Gay Bars."

"We run a legitimate joint . . .": Truscott, "Gay Power Comes to Sheridan Square."

"I was very angry . . .": Crosby, "The Stonewall Riot Remembered."

"We are the Stonewall girls . . .":": Truscott, "Gay Power Comes to Sheridan Square."

"Liberate the street!": Carter, *Stonewall*, 186.

"Christopher Street belongs to the queens!": Carter, *Stonewall*, 183.

"Catch them!": Carter, *Stonewall*, 193.

"'Gay power' erected its brazen head . . .": Truscott, "Gay Power Comes to Sheridan Square."

Chapter Eight—Gay Pride

"To those who wrote . . .": Van Buren, "Dear Abby."

"Did you hear about what's going on . . .": Rodwell, Oral history interviews, Folder 2, 29.

"the fight for the liberation . . .": Marty Robinson Collection.

"Hi, Mom!" and "I am a lesbian and I am beautiful.": Carter, *Stonewall*, 255.

"Everything you think we are . . .": Black, "A Happy Birthday for Gay Liberation."

"Out of the closets and into the streets." "Gay Power." and "Two, four, six, eight . . .": Skir, "Notes from the Underground: The Road That Is Known," 74.

"Three, five, seven, nine . . .": Marty Robinson collection, undated "Gay-In" flyer published by the Gay Activists Alliance.

"The faces of the crowd show no . . .": Skir, "Notes from the Underground: The Road That Is Known," 74.

"As we rolled up Sixth Avenue . . .": Rodwell, Oral history interviews, Folder 2, 90.

"Please let there be more than ten . . .": *Stonewall Uprising* transcript, 31.

"This was the moment when the closet door . . .": "After Stonewall."

"You can cure yourself . . .": Skir, "Notes from the Underground: The Road That Is Known," 74.

"Come out, come out, come out . . .": *Milk*, bonus footage interview with Frank Robinson.

"If a bullet should enter my brain . . .": Shilts, *The Mayor of Castro Street*, 372.

Chapter Nine—Gay Plague

"Everyone detected with AIDS . . .": Buckley, "Crucial Steps in Combating the Aids Epidemic."

"The poor homosexuals . . .": Buchanan, "AIDS disease: It's Nature Striking Back."

"Praise God for AIDS.": *SCLC Magazine* photo spread, 22.

"We die. They do nothing! . . .": "Protesters Call for More Help for Homeless Who Have AIDS," *New York Times*.

"History will recall, Reagan and Bush . . .": ACT UP Ashes Action.

"I have a vision . . .": Hirshman, *Victory*, 224.

"When I was in the military . . .": McDarrah, *Gay Pride*, photograph, 154.

Chapter Ten—The Rainbow

"We, the people, declare today . . .": Obama, "Second Inaugural Address."

"Gilbert, we need a logo." "This will be the most important . . ." and "And it was.": *Milk*, bonus feature "Marching for Equality."

"For if we are truly created equal . . .": Obama, "Second Inaugural Address."

"There has been much to-do . . .": *Stonewall Uprising* transcript, 18.

"We'll be gay until everyone has forgotten . . .": Wittman.

"They were kids. You knew . . .": *Stonewall Uprising* transcript, 32.

"If what I did helped gay people . . .": Hevesi, "Seymour Pine Dies at 91."

"Stonewall happens every day . . .": Apuzzo, Biography: Stonewall Participants.

"stigma attached to being gay" "the major reason . . ." and "I hope we're going to go . . .": Gittings, Interview conducted by Wayne Curtis.

"I have just marched through a little tunnel . . .":Skir, "Notes from the Underground: The Road That Is Known," 75.

BIBLIOGRAPHY

ACT UP Ashes Action. Documentary Footage, October 11, 1992. https://www.youtube.com/watch?v=bWbzinqIlPk

After Stonewall. Documentary film directed by John Scagliotti. New York: First Run Features, 1999.

Altman, Lawrence K. "New Homosexual Disorder Worries Health Officials." *New York Times*, May 11, 1982.

_____. "Rare Cancer Seen in 41 Homosexuals." *New York Times*, July 3, 1981.

Apuzzo, Virginia. Biography: Stonewall Participants. http://www.pbs.org/wgbh/americanexperience/features/biography/stonewall-participants/

Barbara Gittings and Kay Tobin Lahusen gay history papers and photographs. Manuscripts and Archives Division. The New York Public Library. Astor, Lenox, and Tilden Foundations.

Before Stonewall. Documentary film directed by Greta Schiller and Robert Rosenberg. New York: First Run Features, 1984.

Bird, David. "Police Continuing Inquiry on Trees," *New York Times*, July 16, 1969.

_____. "Queens Resident Says the Police Stood By as Park Trees Were Cut," *New York Times*, July 2, 1969.

_____. "Trees in a Queens Park Cut Down as Vigilantes Harass Homosexuals," *New York Times*, July 1, 1969.

Black, Jonathan. "A Happy Birthday for Gay Liberation." *Village Voice*, July 2, 1970, pp. 1, 58.

Brody, Jane. "A Quiet Revolution in Mental Care," *New York Times*, May 19, 1968.

Buchanan, Patrick J. "AIDS disease: It's Nature Striking Back." *New York Post*, May 24, 1983.

Buckley, Jr., William F. "Crucial Steps in Combating the Aids Epidemic; Identify All the Carriers." *New York Times*, March 18, 1986.

Bullough, Vern. L., editor. *Before Stonewall: Activists for Gay and Lesbian Rights in Historical Culture*. New York: Harrington Park Press, 2002.

Carter, David. *Stonewall: The Riots That Sparked the Gay Revolution*. New York: St. Martin's Press, 2004; St. Martin's Griffin edition, 2010.

_____. "An Analytical Collation of Accounts and Documents Recorded in the Year 1969 Concerning the Stonewall Riots." Compiled 1999–2009. Available through author website.

Chan, Sewell. "Images from the Stonewall Uprising's Final Night." *New York Times*, June 1, 2009.

_____. "Venerable Bookstore to Close in Village." *New York Times*, February 3, 2009.

Christopher Street Liberation Day Committee records. Manuscripts and Archives Division. The New York Public Library. Astor, Lenox, and Tilden Foundations.

"Cop Injured 5 Seized in Village." *New York Post*, July 3, 1969.

"Craig L. Rodwell, 52, Pioneer for Gay Rights." *New York Times*, June 20, 1993.

Craig Rodwell papers. Manuscripts and Archives Division. The New York Public Library. Astor, Lenox, and Tilden Foundations.

Crosby, Tina. "The Stonewall Riot Remembered." Term paper dated January 16, 1974. Craig Rodwell papers. Manuscripts and Archives Division. The New York Public Library. Astor, Lenox, and Tilden Foundations.

D'Arcangelo, Angelo. *The Homosexual Handbook*. New York: Ophelia Press, 1969.

Di Brienza, Ronnie. "Stonewall Incident." *The East Village Other*, Vol. 4, No. 32, July 9, 1969.

Eskow, Dennis. "3 Cops Hurt as Bar Raid Riles Crowd," *New York Sunday News*, June 29, 1969.

"Federal Vigilance on Perverts Asked." *New York Times*, December 16, 1950.

Forsythe, Ronald. "Why Can't 'We' Live Happily Ever After, Too?" *New York Times*, February 23, 1969.

Fosburgh, Lacey. "Thousands of Homosexuals Hold a Protest Rally in Central Park." *New York Times*, June 29, 1970, pp. 1, 20.

Fox, Margalit. "Barbara Gittings, 74, Prominent Gay Rights Activist Since '50s, Dies." *New York Times*, March 15, 2007.

Gittings, Barbara. Interview conducted by Wayne Curtis, November 16, 1991. Barbara Gittings and Kay Tobin Lahusen gay history papers and photographs. Manuscripts and Archives Division. The New York Public Library. Astor, Lenox, and Tilden Foundations.

Grutzner, Charles. "Court Annuls S.L.A. Penalty in a Morals Case," *New York Times*, March 9, 1967.

_____. "Mafia Buys Clubs for Homosexuals." *New York Times*, November 30, 1967.

_____. "S.L.A. Won't Act Against Bars Refusing Service to Deviates." *New York Times*, April 26, 1966.

Gunnison, Foster. Undated interview conducted by Martin Duberman. Martin B. Duberman papers. Manuscripts and Archives Division. The New York Public Library. Astor, Lenox, and Tilden Foundations.

Heritage of Pride Records. See finding aid for collection 86, The Lesbian, Gay, Bisexual & Transgender Community Center, New York City.

Hevesi, Dennis. "Seymour Pine Dies at 91; Led Raid on Stonewall Inn." *New York Times*, September 7, 2010, p. 6.

Hirshman, Linda. *Victory: The Triumphant Gay Revolution*. New York: HarperCollins Publishers, 2012.

"Homosexuals Hold Protest in 'Village' After Raid Nets 167." *New York Times*, March 9, 1970.

"Homosexuals' Parade Marks 10th Year of Rights Drive." *New York Times*, June 25, 1979.

Johnson, Haynes. "1968 Democratic Convention: The Bosses Strike Back." *Smithsonian Magazine*, August 2008.

Johnson, Thomas A. "3 Deviates Invite Exclusion by Bars." *New York Times*, April 22, 1966.

Lanigan-Schmidt, Thomas. "Stonewall: Statement of Remembrance," dated 1989. Martin B. Duberman papers. The New York Public Library. Astor, Lenox, and Tilden Foundations.

LeDuff, Charlie. "Participation in Pride Parade Marks Greater Acceptance for the Blue and the Gay." *New York Times*, June 30, 1996.

Leitsch, Dick (aka Price Dickinson). "Gay Riots in the Village." *New York Mattachine Newsletter*, August 1969.

Levin, Jay. "The Gay Anger Behind the Riots." *New York Post*, July 8, 1969, p. 36.

Lisker, Jerry. "Homo Nest Raided, Queen Bees Are Stinging Mad." *New York Sunday News*, July 6, 1969.

Lyons, Richard D. "Psychiatrists, in a Shift, Declare Homosexuality No Mental Illness." *New York Times*, December 16, 1973.

Manford, Morty. "Stonewall Remembrances," written circa 1978. Morty Manford papers. Manuscripts and Archives Division. The New York Public Library. Astor, Lenox, and Tilden Foundations.

Martin B. Duberman papers. Manuscripts and Archives Division. The New York Public Library. Astor, Lenox, and Tilden Foundations.

Marty Robinson Collection. National History Archive. The Lesbian, Gay, Bisexual & Transgender Community Center, New York City.

McDarrah, Fred W., and Timothy S. McDarrah. *Gay Pride: Photographs from Stonewall to Today*. Chicago: a cappella books, Chicago Review Press, 1994.

McGill, Douglas C. "Homosexuals' Parade Dedicated to AIDS Victims." *New York Times*, June 27, 1983.

Milk. Film directed by Gus Van Sant. Focus Features, 2008.

Morty Manford papers. Manuscripts and Archives Division. The New York Public Library. Astor, Lenox, and Tilden Foundations.

"The Night They Raided the Stonewall." *Gay Activist*, June 1971, Vol. 1, No. 3.

"No Place for Gaiety." *New York Post*, June 29, 1969.

"N.Y. Homosexuals Protest Raids." *Washington Post*, July 1, 1969.

Obama, Barack. "Second Inaugural Address." The White House Blog, January 21, 2013. http://www.whitehouse.gov/blog/2013/01/21/second-inauguration-barack-obama

"Perverts Called Government Peril." *New York Times*, April 19, 1950.

"Pickets Aid Homosexuals." *New York Times*, July 5, 1967.

Pileggi, Nicholas. "'Gestapo' or 'Elite'?—The Tactical Patrol Force." *New York Times* (Sunday magazine), July 21, 1968.

"Police Again Rout 'Village' Youths." *New York Times*, June 30, 1969.

"Poll Indicates Majority Favor Quarantine for AIDS Victims." *New York Times*, December 20, 1985.

"Protesters Call for More Help for Homeless Who Have AIDS." *New York Times*, October 8, 1989.

"Queen Power: Fags Against Pigs in Stonewall Bust." *RAT*, Vol. 2, No. 14, July 9–23, 1969, p. 6.

Rodwell, Craig. "Get the Mafia and the Cops out of Gay Bars." Privately published with Homophile Youth Movement, June 28, 1969.

_____. Oral history interviews collected by Martin Duberman, 1990. Craig Rodwell papers. Manuscripts and Archives Division. The New York Public Library. Astor, Lenox, and Tilden Foundations.

Russo, Vito. "Why I'm Not Marching." *New York Native*, June 20–July 3, 1983.

Schmalz, Jeffrey. "The 1992 Elections: The States—the Gay Issues." *New York Times*, November 5, 1992, p. 11.

Schmeck, Jr., Harold M. "Psychiatrists Approve Change on Homosexuals." *New York Times*, April 9, 1974.

Schott, Webster. "A 4-Million Minority Asks for Equal Rights." *New York Times*, November 12, 1967.

SCLC Magazine. March/April 1987, photo spread p. 22.

Shilts, Randy. *And the Band Played On: Politics, People, and the AIDS Epidemic*. New York: St. Martin's Press, 1987; twentieth anniversary edition, 2007.

_____. *The Mayor of Castro Street: The Life and Times of Harvey Milk*. New York: St. Martin's Press, 1982.

Skir, Leo. "Notes from the Underground: The Road That Is Known." *Evergreen Review*, No. 82, September 1970, pp. 16, 18, 20, 74–75.

Smith, Howard. "Full Moon over the Stonewall." *Village Voice*, July 3, 1969.

Stolberg, Sheryl Gay. "Obama Signs Away 'Don't Ask, Don't Tell.'" *New York Times*, December 22, 2010, p. 12.

Stonewall Uprising. A Q-Ball Productions documentary film for *American Experience*, WGBH Educational Foundation, 2011. Transcript available online.

Strong, Lester. "Stonewall 25: Reflections on a Silver Anniversary." *Out*, June 1994, pp. 6–7, 36, 42.

Summer of Love. A Franco Dolgin Productions Film for *American Experience* in association with KQED. WGBH Educational Foundation, 2007. Transcript available online.

Taylor, Jr., Stuart. "High Court, 5-4, Says States Have the Right to Outlaw Private Homosexual Acts." *New York Times*, July 1, 1986.

The Times of Harvey Milk. Documentary film directed by Robert Epstein. The Criterion Collection, 1984.

Truscott IV, Lucian. "Gay Power Comes to Sheridan Square." *Village Voice*, July 3, 1969.

Van Buren, Abigail. "Dear Abby." *New York Post*, February 9, 1971.

Williams, Lena. "200,000 March in Capital to Seek Gay Rights and Money for AIDS." *New York Times*, October 12, 1987.

Wittman, Carl. "A Gay Manifesto." Gay Flames Pamphlet No. 9, published through the New York Gay Liberation Front.

A NOTE ABOUT THE PHOTOGRAPHS

Most news media outlets paid little attention to the unrest triggered by a pre-dawn raid at a gay bar in New York City on June 28, 1969. As a result, few photographs document the events in and around the Stonewall Inn that came to be seen as seminal moments in gay rights history. Available images and supplemental quotes help *Stonewall*'s readers visualize the events captured in this book's text. In a few cases, some Stonewall photos are presented out of chronological sequence with the narrative; dates and captions identify all of these instances.

PHOTO CREDITS

INDEX

Note: Page numbers in *italics* refer to illustrations.